Fortunella

RONALD WHITE

NEWMAN SPRINGS PUBLISHING
320 Broad Street
Red Bank, NJ 07701

First originally published by Newman Springs Publishing 2022

ISBN 978-1-63881-571-6 (Paperback)
ISBN 978-1-63881-572-3 (Digital)

Printed in the United States of America

PREFACE

The following story is fiction. I could say it's true but who would believe that. I have compressed in time some of the events to make the story flow. There are gaps in time that are not important to the story and will be filled in at a later time in the narrative. Most of the names are real, sort of, unless characters lied to me about their name, which happened more often than not. If I have offended anyone by using their names, please accept my apologies and thanks. It would not have been the same without you. Time removes much of the seriousness of life and, hopefully, installs more humor than guilt. Some of the "fellas," a Bahamian euphemism for "guys," and some of the Miami "businessmen," well you know, used their real names, and I do not want to piss them off, so I did change their names. It's a shame I had to do that because they were great stage names.

Dauber

And then one day, I had a job to do
Down below bridge, by where the docks begin,
And there I saw a clipper towing through,
Up from the sea that morning, entering in.
Raked to the nines, she was lofty and thin,
Her ensign ruffling red, her bunts in a pile,
Beauty and strength together, wonder, and style.
She docked close to the gates, and there she lay
Over the water from me, well insight;
And as I worked I watched her all the day,
Finding her beauty ever fresh delight.
Her house flag was bright green with strips of white.

High in the sunny air it rose to shake
Above the skysail poles' most splendid rake
And when I felt unhappy, I would look
Over the river at her and her pride,
So calm so quiet, came as a rebuke
To half the passionate pathways which I tried;
And though the autumn ran its term and died,
And winter fell and cold December came,
She was still splendid there and still the same.
Then on a day she sailed; but when she went
My mind was clear on what I had to try;
To see the sea and ships and what they meant,
That was the thing I longed to do; so I
Drew and worked hard and studied and put by,
And thought of nothing else but that one end,
But let all else go hang—love, money, friend.

John Masefield

THE BEGINNING

Terpenes, an organic chemical given off by trees in the southern Appalachians that causes the haze or smoke for which the Great Smoky Mountains were named. I never looked it up, but according to Mike, a college friend and teacher of seventh graders at Elkins Junior High, it's why the mountains are commonly shrouded. The sound of hammered dulcimers, Gibson guitars, and fiddles wells up and drifts across the treetops. I loved the time I spent there in college and part of my time ashore in the '70s, but the sky is small, captured by the hills. I am a sailor. I long for the sea and its sky, horizon to horizon, hills of clouds and blue. Every color of blue beyond even what my imagination can conjure.

After three years in a magic mountain town in northern West Virginia, working as a wildlife biologist for the US Fish and Wildlife Service, I was ready to move back. Sitting steeped in bureaucracy, I longed for the openness and freedom of my former life aboard an oceangoing sailboat. Nine-to-five for three years was enough. I tendered my resignation and sent letters by plane, freight boat, and all-terrain vehicle to an old friend on a small island in a big blue sea. He needed a manager for a small research and educational foundation located about six hundred miles southeast of Miami. Reefs, sand, exotic biota, a great escape from the terpenes.

Chuck and I had met in a dive shop in the Florida Keys in the mid-'60s. He had just graduated from Annapolis, and I was a college freshman on spring break. I needed a dive buddy, and Chuck and his buddy had rented a boat for a reef dive off Key Largo. We buddied up and spent the next week diving the Keys and, on a mad overnight drive upstate, dove the springs of northern Florida. After this whirlwind dive vacation, we communicated several times by mail and then went on with our lives.

By the early '70s, I was a science teacher in a hospital-based nursing school. I instructed scuba on the side. I walked into a local dive shop one day to get my tanks filled and noticed a pair of tanks with Chuck's name written on the top of the tank. Slightly bewildered by this coincidence, I wrote my name and phone number on a Posta note and stuck it on the tank. Several days later, I received a call from Chuck. He told me he was teaching diving at UConn and also finishing a master's in ecology and was also working on a sailboat in Mystic, Connecticut.

My love of diving started the summer of my junior year in high school. My mom, through a high school friend, got me a job at the Straightsmouth Inn in Rockport, Massachusetts. I was the chief dishwasher for a five-star restaurant. I shared a room in a small cottage reserved for all the service people employed by the inn. Most of the crew were college students from BU and Cornell. The cottage was right on Thatcher's Cove, a boulder-rimmed lagoon of clear jewel-green frigid water, full of lobster and flounder. Having a taste for both, I decided to snorkel around and investigate the wildlife. After ten minutes, I gave up and headed for a hot shower.

What I had seen was beautiful, but the water was intolerably cold. My dishwashing pardoner told me I could buy a wet suit and dive gear in Beverly, just a short train ride from Rockport.

I hoped on my bike the next day and headed to the train station for a journey to New England Divers. The commuter train dropped me off at Beverly, and I quickly found my way to the dive shop. The staff suited me up with a tank, regulator, buoyancy vest, flippers, mask, and a full wet suit. The suit included a hood, Farmer John pants, top, booties, and gloves. The weight belt weighed in at eighteen pounds. The last item was a three-band speargun big enough to kill Jaws. I stepped out of the fitting room with the entire suit on, put the tank on my back, and threw my clothes into a dive bag and paid the man in cash. As I walked out the door, the salesman asked if I was going to drive home with all that gear on? I turned and told him I was taking the train.

The trek to the train station was entertaining for the towns-folk. It remained entertaining for the commuters on the train. The Schwinn 10 speed was not the bike for a fully clothed diver with gear and a speargun, but with great effort, I made it back to the bunkhouse.

The next day, I was chomping at the bit to immerse myself into that jewel-green water and see what wildlife I could collect. The glacial boulders went right down to the water's edge. It was a seal entry down the slippery rock face into the water. The fringed ocean seeped into my wet suit and warmed quickly, just like the man in the shop said it would.

Twelve feet down, I met my first lobster. My three-fingered gloves closed around his carapace, and I slid him into my net bag. An immense flounder lay on a pure sand bottom, adjusting his color scheme to match his background. My speargun was loaded with one rubber, which seemed appropriate for such an easy target. The spear went completely through the fish and into the sand bottom a foot. I continued to collect lobsters until I figured I had enough to feed all my workmates.

I had become disoriented at the bottom of the cove and decided to surface and get my bearings. Coming up from twenty-five feet, I noticed a boat directly above me and swam at an angle to avoid hitting the bottom of the hull. My hooded head broke the surface right next to a white gleaming sailboat hull sitting right in the middle of the cove.

A young woman leaned over the rail and asked me what I was doing in such cold water. I responded that I was diving for lobsters and flounder. She asked me if I would like to come aboard and have a drink. I had never been on a yacht, so I took my tank and weight belt off and handed it to the woman's friend and climbed aboard. My hood came off, and I took in the view of my surroundings. We sat dead center in the cove with a landscape of ancient stone homes, massive boulders, and cliffs. Seagulls painted the air, with white wings swooping near the boat in hopes of food. The lobsters in the net bag cracked and clicked their ancient carapaces together, and the flounder slapped his big tail enough that the bag jumped around the floor of the cockpit.

So this is a yacht, I thought to myself. The young woman was covering me with questions about lobster-catching, but my mind was creating a life scenario that included sailboats and diving in much-warmer water.

We cooked the fish and some of the lobsters and drank beer and sat in the cockpit of the yacht, with the sun sparkling on the water. That moment was the opening act for the rest of my life. I quit a dozen career-path jobs and women to reach that moment again and again.

Chuck and I met at the boatyard and swapped yarns about the intervening years. This friendship morphed into a partnership between the boat and our dreams. Chuck moved his Winnebago to my place, and we began to plan a circumnavigation in the boat. This would include lots of diving and adventure.

In the ensuing year, we read every book we could find on voyaging in a small yacht. We eventually gathered two great young women to share the adventure with us and set off for warmer climes. We tried the boat on for size, and it was apparent that a twenty-eight-foot boat was not big enough for four people. There was a decision made to get another boat and share the dream but on separate boats. I found a thirty-six-foot boat, in fairly good shape, and I took out a small loan from the hospital I was employed at, did some tweaking on the rig and engine, and we both left in the fall of 1974. My pardoner, Mary, and I left in late October and worked our way down the East Coast to South Florida, where I, by pure happenstance, acquired a job with the Mote Marine Lab. Mary acquired a job as the local traveling community nurse. We tied up the boat and settled in for a while to make some money and enjoy a Florida winter.

Chuck and his girlfriend, Kathy, left late and had a chilly trip until they arrived in Florida. Mary and I drove over to Miami and celebrated our mutual accomplishment. I told Chuck that I could not give up the chance to work with Eugenia Clark, Jacque Cousteau, John Lillie, and many other world-class scientists. I would be working with shark experts, bird experts, and continuing research on red tide. This was my bailiwick, and I wanted to stretch out this experience as much as possible. My degree was in invertebrate zoology, not nursing-school microbiology.

Chuck and Kathy were excited for us. They remained steadfast on their journey as planned. The reality was, they stuck to the journey and waited for a plan to congeal. We went sailing in Biscayne Bay for the day and wished Chuck and Kathy great adventures.

Chuck and Kathy sailed straight out through the Bahamas into the Atlantic. This was definitely the hard way. The next landfall was southeast, for as long as you could stand six-foot waves over the bow. They lasted six hundred miles before they pulled into South Caicos. They were punished enough. South Caicos was a third-world village with a first-world hotel, US Coast Guard Loran station, and an old US Air Force runway. They had fresh water delivered by donkey cart, regular food deliveries from Miami, and a good harbor. They decided to stay.

While I was back in Florida, rubbing shoulders with the biological greats at Mote, Chuck was busy looking for a place to do his own shoulder-rubbing. He started by sailing across the Caicos Bank to a small island named Pine Cay. The island had been recently purchased by a couple from Vermont. They planned to bring wealthy folks from the States, down to paradise, and establish a small development on an eight-hundred-acre island. Bill and Jennie liked Chuck and Kathy and agreed to sell them a small piece of land overlooking the harbor. Chuck, being a natural builder, anchored the boat in the harbor and started a house. Bill and Jenny thought it would be a great idea to offer the prospective homeowners an environmental conscience. That conscience was two biology majors prepared to start and operate a nonprofit research and educational foundation. Chuck gave it the acronym the Foundation for PRIDE. Pride was short for Preserve Reefs and Islands from Development and Exploitation.

Meanwhile, Mary and I had spent almost three years in Florida, and Mary missed Mystic and her family. We decided to sail *Vamos*, our boat, back to New England and sell the boat and regroup. We had a great ride home, arriving in early summer. Mary got a job right away, but it was not so easy for a marine biologist to secure employment. The next winter, Chuck sent me a letter asking if I would come to the island and perform an environmental survey. I left on the next plane for Providenciales in the Turks and Caicos. That done, I returned to a rather disgruntled wife, who had made plans without me. I sold the boat, packed my old pickup full of nautical stuff, and headed west. My first stop was Elkins, West Virginia, to visit an old college buddy. After a week of carousing around, I opened the local paper and found an ad for an environmental biologist position with the Fish and Wildlife Service. It was another job I could not turn down. I bought a forty-acre farm with the boat money and waited for Chuck to make me another offer. It took two years for Chuck to get the wherewithal to write me another letter, but when it came, I sold the farm, quit my job, and got in my old truck and headed for Miami.

I was instructed, in Chuck's letter, to make myself at home in my friend's three-room condo in South Miami and secure my truck for medium-term storage. I left it in the condo parking lot. The next day, I made my way, by taxi, to Miami International Airport for an early-morning flight to Providenciales in the Turks and Caicos Islands. England has been trading with and educating these islands since the Spanish moved on to more fertile ground. America has given them a dollar-based economy and an insatiable market for green, aromatic, hallucinogenic trade goods. Not homegrown, just traveling to a friendly shore with airports, the English language, American dollars, aviation gas, and an entrepreneurial native population.

I stepped off a DC-6 onto the rock runway, the edge of which was littered with the bones of at least six aircraft. Not passenger flights but abortive attempts to land with no fuel or no landing lights, or just too much cargo and not enough skill. A smuggler's paradise!

The customs agent smiled at me when I told him I was visiting Pine Cay.

"That will be a rough ride through the reef today, mon."

"How big is the boat?" I asked.

"Big enough, but the sea is bigger."

He gave me a big smile and stamped my passport. I arrived at the boat about 5:00 p.m. It was an old Trojan. I used to work on wooden boats like this one when I was in graduate school. The bottoms were always loose because the bronze screws were trying to revert to their natural state—copper, zinc, and nickel. Once they become divorced, the planks gained a mind of their own.

I was aware of all that as the boat hit the first eight-foot wave crossing into about six thousand feet of water. The Brits had blasted a hole in the barrier reef to facilitate transportation. The waves from the Atlantic love to climb through that hole. The boat settled onto the next wave and forged on. This had become an adventure; the screws were still holding, and the boat was thrashing through a dark wonderful sea.

Kathy and Chuck Hesse had been carving out a niche for the last six years on this semiarid cay, populated with a cross section of new-world humanity. The inhabitants were homesteaders from pre-Communist Russia, speculators from the States, ancestors of shipwrecked slaves, and the ever-present Brits.

Everyone had a slightly different agenda with the English language as the only common ground. The Russians arrived with a land grant from the English Crown and promised to employ as many natives as possible. The Russians were slow and deliberate, building in the arid jungle, small and private. No generators, just kerosene lights and refrigeration, when the freight boat came with enough to fill the fuel barrel. Little money was invested, so nothing was imperative.

The facts were always a bit confusing to me, the newcomer. I was told a minister of trade from Grand Turk had started a small hotel to encourage tourism and development. A small airstrip and a good harbor slowly attracted the proper money-bearing tourists with visions of owning a little bit of paradise. A large check was finely written to someone, for a commonly known sum, to secure about half the acreage on the island. The island was to be subdivided into large ecologically sound, extremely expensive building lots. All unusable land was to be left as parkland. Sound familiar? The Hesse's niche, their biological bend, was attached firmly to the ecological elbow of the developer, Bill and Jenny. Not that that is a bad thing.

The gentile prospective land buyers were all members of the National Audubon Society, the World Wildlife Fund, and the local garden club back in the States, and always caught the most-recent episode of the *Undersea World of Jacques Cousteau*. A young idealistic couple, Chuck and Kathy, well educated in engineering and biology, gave everyone a sense of ecological well-being. They were encouraged to start a tax-exempt nonprofit educational foundation to protect the environment and educate local native children and adults about the pitfalls of overfishing. College students were also on the menu as a potential for in situ education and tanning during winter and spring breaks. This influx of money and fertile minds was the reason for my arrival.

SETTLING IN

The old Trojan rolled beam to beam, as we ran broadside to the sea for about four nautical miles north, up the coast to Pine Cay. I could see one small light on the starboard beam. That was it; the rest was starlight, no GPS or loran. Not even an RDF. Just time, compass-bearing, and speed equals distance and dead-reckoned location. All I could see through the windshield were the waves slapping against the portside of the boat as the red running light painted the spray over the port bow. Best to just let the captain do his job. I closed my eyes and held on. It had been a long day from Miami to Pine Cay.

The boat turned to starboard and began surfing down some good-size waves. *We must be in shallow water again*, I thought. The light was on the starboard bow now, and we were closing in. We eased around the dark shadow of an island and motored slowly along a rocky shore.

The radio came alive with a familiar voice.

Where were the lights?

"John, is that you?"

"Yeah, Chuck! Can you grab a line?"

The boat backed down, and the prop wash kicked the stern to starboard. I was there! I could see my friend Chuck leaning over to take my bags into his world. A golf cart arrived to carry the other passengers up to the hotel.

I stood on the dock in the dark and watched the old powerboat pull off to return to Provo. Nobody ever says Providenciales, except the conquistador who named it. There were still no lights except a kerosene lamp at the head of the dock. Chuck grabbed my seabag and motioned for me to follow. We walked along a sandy trail for about ten minutes until a warm glow of light illuminated the leaves and branches that were around the entranceway to a small house.

"Is the light source kerosene?" I asked.

"No, it's solar."

"How's that work?"

"I bought some solar-voltaic panels from Edmund Scientific and put them on the roof. The panels convert photons into electrons that we store in batteries to run our twelve-volt lights. It won't run much, but the reading lights are nice when the sun goes down."

"What does the rest of the island use?"

"A very big diesel generator for the hotel and the rest of the houses on the island. Kathy and I are willing to live with kerosene refrigeration, solar hot water, and solar lighting. Our stove is propane. It's pretty simple, except for the Coleman lampwick on the fridge. It's a mess to change, and we run out of them all the time. We buy them by the case when we are in Miami.

"As soon as the wind generator arrives, I plan to switch over to a twelve-volt refer. The one at the lab is making so much power our golf cart batteries are blowing up from overcharging, faster than we can replace them."

"You mean you have too much power?"

"In a word, yes, for the time being. We will never need air-conditioning as long as the trades keep blowing. Twelve-volt refrigeration would keep enough load on the power supply to keep the batteries from being overcharged and free us from the maintenance of kerosene refrigeration. Shipping batteries and kerosene from Miami takes six weeks and a lot of paperwork."

I bedded down on a small cot right off the kitchen and fell fast asleep. The next day promised to bring sunshine and new wonders. Kathy was the first person to stir the next morning. She was a tall slim sandy-haired woman with freckles and a nice smile. She met Chuck and me on a dive trip to a lake in northern Connecticut in the winter. Chuck was teaching a dive course in underwater research techniques at UConn and invited me to help with his students on the rather-unusual trip. There were ten of us in a Winnebago parked on a frozen lakeshore. Researchers from UConn were attempting to harvest and collect the eggs of landlocked salmon. As the dive support, we were there to photograph the underwater process and then eat as much salmon as we could. Winter diving in a snowstorm was challenging and a bit crazy.

Both Chuck and I intuitively realized that any of the girls on this trip were not the tea-and-crumpet type and were open for great adventure. We were building a sailboat to go on a great adventure, and Kathy had all the attributes of a coparticipant. Kathy and Chuck were both working on master's degrees in the field of ecology at the time. She had not decided on a thesis at that point but would soon do so in a remote spot called South Caicos. That was where she and Chuck landed on the very same sailboat that Chuck and I were working on at the time. That dive trip started their relationship that continued on to marriage and a little house overlooking a beautiful patch of crystal-clear blue water on Pine Cay.

"Do you want peanut butter and jelly on your toast or just butter?" Kathy said.

"All three," I said. "Where did you get the bread?"

"The cook for the construction crew makes it fresh every day. I have to remember to put in my order. The crew will be here today. They sail over from North Caicos on Monday morning. You will know when they sail into the harbor. They make a hellacious noise at the end of the race."

"What race?"

"They sail over here in three thirty-foot handmade boats, and as you know, if there are two or more sailboats within sight of one another, it's a race. Although this is a little different from the average yacht club event."

I walked out to the deck overlooking a deep-blue ribbon of clear warm water. I could see the sails of the native sloops working their way along the edge of the mangroves. These boats have changed little in the last two hundred years. Except for a few minor alterations, they hadn't changed much in the last thousands of years.

Every time the lead boat would tack and cross the bow of the second boat, a hail of water would be released from each boat in an attempt to fill the other boat and slow it down. Half the crew on each boat were throwing water at their opponent. This looked more like a riot than a race. It then dawned on me that I might have something to learn from these fellas that I had come to teach. How many people get to sail/race to work while singin' and yellin' at one another and the Lord? The Lord is with them, always.

I looked back at Kathy. She saw how much this race had impressed me. The bread was better than I imagined. Fresh, soft, sweet with a nice thick crust as a border. This was the beginning of a long friendship. I thanked her for the slice and walked back into the kitchen. The rest of the breakfast was Tang, nonfat powdered milk, and Taster's Choice coffee. I was to learn that all our food came in boxes, jars, or cans. If you wanted fresh, you went fishin'. Not that that was a bad thing. In fact, that was a great thing.

"Hello," said Chuck, "are you ready for your first day?"

"I'm ready for anything. When do we get to it?"

"As soon as we help the crew get the boats up on the beach."

Chuck, Kathy, and I pushed our way through the thick undergrowth and out onto the crushed coral sand. My bare toes merged with the organic beach. The crushed exoskeletons and coral from countless marine animals now formed the white sandbox of every developer's dreams. Chuck and I were more interested in the origins of the beach than how many dollars per lineal foot we could sell it for. That is the difference between a scientist and an entrepreneur.

The native sloops made one last tack and headed for the landing beach. The fellas jumped out as the boat stem hit the sand. Logs were rolled down the beach and nudged against the bow of each boat. It was all pushing and pulling until the wood (I would say wooden, but they don't) boats were well up on the beach. The boats would lie there until Friday, the next race day.

Chuck and I left the construction crew to their boats and walked along the shore toward several small buildings and what looked like a sixty-foot tower with a wind generator on it. Kathy went back to the house with plans to meet us at the conch shack for more education on the conch lifestyle.

"Is that what I think it is?"

"Yup, it's one big California wind generator, six-thousand bucks' worth, plus the batteries and all the switches. We're running our wet lab with it. It's 120 volts' house current. The sixty cycles part doesn't start until the wind is blowin' at least fifteen knots. Life is full of wrinkles, and that is a big one. The 12-volt unit we are putting on the dome is direct current. It starts charging at nine knots. If we want to make AC (alternating current) out of that power, we have to run it through an inverter to jack it up to 120 volts and throw some cycles into it, and viola, we are back to running big stuff. The conversion produces a lot of heat, and that is wasted energy."

At this point, I was pulling heavily on college physics and realizing that this whole operation was the beginning of a whole new phase of my trip on planet Earth. Chuck, the engineer, and Kathy, the biologist, had created their own little tropical commune, and I was about to become their front man.

DOMES AMERICA

I spent the next few weeks becoming more familiar with the lay of the island. Pine Cay is about a mile long by half-a-mile wide. The south end is a blind pass that has filled in with a narrow finger of sand connecting it to Little Water Cay.

It is in a sweet spot, so to speak. It lies on the northwest corner of a broken circle of islands with a diameter of eighty miles or so. The shallow bank of sand, with coral heads and more conch than a galaxy of stars, is in the center of this narrow ribbon of emergent coral rock called the Caicos Islands. Pine Cay is the only place in the island chain that has a sizable freshwater lens. This is an archaic subterrain pool of water captured in porous rock. The denser salt water surrounding the island keeps this precious freshwater supply from slipping away. There are seven freshwater ponds scattered around Pine Cay, providing a unique ecological landscape. The rest of the island chain receives about twenty inches of rain per year. Pine Cay's geographical position lends itself to an annual rainfall of about twice the rest of the islands. That is what I call a sweet spot. Oh, I forgot, the pine trees are short and stunted. These need a little water; none of the other islands have any pine trees at all.

Pine Cay's population consisted of two Russians, one Brit, seven Americans, and a weekly influx of islanders to build houses and work in the hotel. The Meridian Club, with a restaurant, bar, swimming pool, and six cabanas, occupied the oceanfront beach about halfway down the island. The Russian's cabin was near the south end of the island, and Chuck's world was on the north end. A central road connected them all together by golf cart or an unhurried walk. These three locations naturally separated the three different philosophical approaches to inhabiting this little eight hundred acres. We were all strategically perched on the 23d parallel, the Tropic of Cancer.

Chuck was deep into building a home for the nonprofit he and Kathy had to set up. My early morning tour included the wet lab, with a large (five foot by twelve foot) table with twelve-inch sides full of sea water and many immature conch. This was the nursery room for the baby snails that they had been collecting from the wild. The research plan was to measure growth rates, experiment with various natural food sources, and search for a way to hatch conch from eggs and then shepherd them through metamorphosis to adult conch.

Chuck explained to me that queen conch were the largest of the vegetarian mollusks in tropical waters. The other big snails, queen helmets, were carnivores and not nearly as tasty. A contingent of workers from Italy arrived in the local islands to harvest the helmets for their shells, about forty years ago. The Italians used them to make cameos. They had already plundered the Mediterranean population. Their plan to do the same in the Caribbean came to a screeching halt when the Italian workers collected the most abundant snail in the water, which was the queen conch. Good to eat but not good for carving into cameos. The whole operation went bust for lack of a lowly biologist to tell them which snail to collect. A nearby island is still cluttered with the machinery, workman housing, and half a million of the wrong shells the Italians left behind.

The next building was the generator shack with all the electrical switches, power inverters, relays, and batteries necessary to keep the wet lab running. The monster wind generator, standing sixty feet above the shack, was busy converting the Coriolis effect and all the air moving back and forth between high and low-pressure systems into electrical energy. All the work being done by electrical motors and lights in the wet lab was powered by the motion of the whirling blades sixty feet above my head and the whirling planet just below our feet. It took three hundred thousand years for our species to figure out that the earth was spinning one thousand miles per hour at the equator. Then we also figured out that the earth was twenty-four thousand nautical miles in circumference. That realization gave us a

15

Ronald White

twenty-four-hour day and a lot of wind above and below the equator we now call the trade winds.

We backed out of the small control shack and started up a small path. I could see what looked like a large shingled basketball rising from the bush.

"What is that?" I said to Chuck.

"It's our geodesic dome."

"That must have taken a few freight-boat trips to get all those two-by-fours and shingles down here."

"It came in a kit," Chuck said. "The local guys have never built a round building before. It's been an interesting learning curve, literally and figuratively. We did it without power tools. Just handsaws and hammers. Fortunately, most of the wood comes already cut. You can help finish the living quarters, that's your new home."

We climbed up the stairs onto the first floor. The front room was three stories high. A stairway led to the second floor that occupied half the circumference of the dome. The office was there. A ladder led up through a hatch onto a landing with a dozen bunks made of two-by-fours and plywood.

"This is our student dorm."

I was humbled by the work that two very idealistic people had done.

The dome had its own smaller wind generator perched just above the peak of the roof. A twenty-foot-by-twelve-foot wing extended out from the main building. It had a galvanized water tank, painted black, standing on wooden legs next to the wing. Chuck confirmed that the tank was our pressure hot water, heated by the sun and pumped up there by the wind. The rainwater was collected off the roof during the infrequent rain showers and captured in large fiberglass water tanks made from four-foot-high sheets of molded fiberglass pulled into a big circle and glued to a piece of the same material laid out flat on the ground. The circle ends were glued and screwed together to form a circular tank that held about four hundred gallons of water. With three of these, we could drink and shower as if we were in the navy. When students were there, we made them pump the water into the tank on the roof with a water pump powered by a

human arm. The student had to wobble the handle back and forth twenty times to pump enough water into the tank to take a short shower. A rope actuated the showerhead. You got wet, soaped up, and rinsed off. Twenty students used twenty gallons.

Kathy stuck her head in the door and told us that a cart was heading to the club for lunch, if we wanted to catch a ride. We jumped on board the five-passenger golf cart and hummed along the sand road, past the airstrip, a private home, and onto the club. The ten-minute ride not only moved us physically about half a mile, but it also moved us philosophically at least a light-year from Chuck and Kathy's world. All motors and lights at this end of the island purred along with current provided the old-fashioned way, by diesel power. Parts and fuel were hauled six hundred miles over water from Miami at great expense. The club heated water by electricity generated with fuel made by bacteria munching on ancient single-celled organisms that settled to the bottom of an ancient ocean millions of years ago. Crude oil was the final product.

It's a good thing it's taken us 290,000 years, the theoretical time *Homo sapiens* have been in existence, to build an internal combustion engine, since it takes so much time to make crude oil. One can hope we will strike a balance between our consumption and nature's production.

As Chuck plugged the golf cart into a gang plug next to the front door, a hitching post for electric cars. I queried him on the power source for the hotel.

"It's old-world stuff," he said. "They even heat the water with electric tank-style water heaters. We're on the tropic of cancer, and they don't use solar, can you believe it?"

"I guess they are living better electrically, the mantra of Florida Power and Light. You have to admit, that mantra worked in Florida. Everybody I know has disconnected their solar hot-water panels and bought an electric water heater.

"Are there any plans to move to solar at this end of the island?"

Chuck was shaking his head.

"Guests want their pink sand, crystal-clear water, and tropical breezes with all the comforts of the burbs. Someday tourists will brag about their eco-friendly vacation on a remote island, but not now, not yet."

We settled into a served lunch. No menu, no options. The food was planned and prepared by Jenny Coles, wife of Bill Coles, apple orchard owners from Vermont. They were the owners of the hotel and most of the island. Jenny handled the food and supplies for the island. Bill's job was to just enjoy the ride. I had met them the first time I came to the island. A lot had changed in the three years I had been away.

After lunch, I was introduced to Nick. He and his wife had been recruited to manage the island. This made Nick the guy responsible for Pine Cay's utilities, roads, and the entire infrastructure. This is a hard job when you have trained employees to help you. It gets much harder when you are the all-in-one guy. I also met Paul. He had come to the island to run the dive operation. This guy, Paul, was a character out of a Bogart film. When I informed him that I was a dive instructor, he eyed me with much suspicion. I backed up mentally and softened my approach. I told him I was ready to hit the water anytime he was ready.

"Can you believe that, another dive instructor?" Paul said. "Now we just need some tourists to instruct."

"Well, I'm not here to step on your niche," I said. "My job is to sell T-shirts and teach biology." I think that settled him a little.

"I'm heading out to the reef this afternoon. Do you want to come?" said Paul.

This was the invitation I was looking for.

"Meet you down at the dock at two," said Paul.

"I'll be there with bells on."

The boat was the strangest dive vessel I had ever seen. Three sealed pontoons sitting under a frame of two-by-sixes and plywood decking, fifteen by thirty feet. A Johnson 50 hp on each stern quarter could push the damn thing along at twenty knots with a dozen people and dive gear. The lifelines were three-quarter-inch galvanized pipe all the way around the boat. There were two swimming pool ladders on the back and an anchor on the bow.

Paul and I arrived at the reef thirty minutes out from the dock. I slipped on my snorkel gear and vaulted over the stern into a swarm of bubbles and liquid air. The water disappeared into a haze of yellow grunts. I was doing my best to remember the common names of every fish in my field of view. Wrasses, snappers, myriads of grunts, angles, gobies, and groupers; look at all the grouper.

Paul slipped by me with a handful of dead fish. A large Nassau grouper slid out of its hole and headed for Paul. This was not their first encounter. Paul released the bait, and the grouper opened wide and inhaled most of it. The slippery dicks and Beau Gregory's got the rest. I hit the surface, grabbed some air, and pressed hard for the bottom. Thirty feet down, I hit the edge of the first step. There was a sheer drop off another fifty feet and so on to the bottom of the world. The crown of the reef was emergent at low tide, with the abyss less than two hundred feet away.

In 1979, the fringe reef was not virgin, but the community was abundant, vibrant, and trusting. This last adjective describes a reef state seldom found thirty years later. The abundance and trust have long since become rare. Spear-fishing pressure, traps, and gill nets have stripped the underwater islands of their diversity and abundance. Each fringe or patch reef operates like a human city. Crustaceans (crabs, shrimp, and lobster), echinoderms (sea cucumbers, starfish, and sea urchins), and all the finfish scurry about, nipping and chewing on one another and the reef itself. The reef (a large group of colonial animals) is, with the help of a partner alga, constantly growing. The rest of the cast is forever involved in breaking the reef down into fine calcium sand.

Stateside sand comes from the mountains via rivers to the sea. The low coral islands of the Caribbean are part of a reef system that makes its own sand on site.

Every twitch of a fin, every snap of a shrimp's claw reverberates through the reef, out onto the turtle grass flats. The modern reef system of today has been tweaking itself since the K2 iridium boundary was laid down sixty-five million years ago. There is little paleontological evidence of any reefs surviving the meteor impact that killed the dinosaurs. Perhaps two or three species of cnidarian (coral animals) survived and populated the modern world with the wonderfully complex interwoven economic system we call a coral reef. About fifty-five million years to do the job. That's a significant investment in time and resources and well worth it, I would say.

Paul had gathered the anchor in, the motors were running, and the bow had fallen off. I asked if we were heading back. He said we had to visit a grass flat and gather several species of macroalgae (multicellular) for the conch lab. Since the conch were not filter feeders, all their fresh food had to be brought from the field. This was just part of the ritual.

We anchored again and quickly hit the water. Paul had given me a pillowcase in which to stuff the conch food. I busied myself scooping up all the loose algae I could find. It was green and fluffy and packed easily into the bags. The turtle grass was firmly rooted to the bottom, just like the grass in your backyard. Roots, stems, leaves, and flowers define a modern angiosperm, a flowering grass. The plants we were gathering were several rungs down the ladder of evolution with no roots or flowers. We did not know what the conch were eating, but it was easier and less damaging to the environment to gather the free-floating vegetation. When you start studying a particular species, everything is a mystery. It took a while just to figure out what and how conch ate.

It turns out conch spend a good part of their day scraping microscopic single-celled algae (epiphytes) off (macrophytes) larger plants. They do all this with a file-like gizmo called a radula. This means that conch consume the fast-reproducing algal cells without harming the slow-growing higher plants they live on. It's a great plan. A primary producer, (single-celled algae), converts solar energy and CO_2 and water into sugars and starches, and the most populous primary consumer on the grass flat (the conch) eats the algal cell and converts it to protein. You can't make protein any easier than that. Sharks, turtles, stingrays, lobsters, and humans all enjoy the benefits of high-quality low-fat protein. The French have been eating snails for hundreds of years. Conch are just larger saltwater cousins. Most of the world's population live on rice, corn, and wheat, all macrophytes. It takes huge quantities of fresh water, fertilizer, and fuel to grow these crops. We then feed them to cattle and sheep to harvest protein for burgers and lamb chops. That is the hard way to make protein from sunlight. The plan, after Chuck and Kathy worked out the life cycle of the conch, was to commercially farm the big snail. Remember I said Kathy was looking for a master's thesis? All this research was the culmination of her curiosity.

Paul ran the flat top up on the beach next to the lab to facilitate unloading the conch food. We sprinkled some of the algae onto the wet table and rinsed off the dive gear. I spotted one more character I hadn't been introduced to yet.

"Hi, I'm Ron."

"Yeah, I know. Chuck has been talking about your arrival for a while, another environmental wacko for this end of the island."

"Are you a right-wing capitalist wacko to balance the scale?"

He broke into a great smile and laughed. "I was just seeing if you had a sense of humor. You will need one if you plan to stay here."

"What's that supposed to mean?" I asked.

"In case you hadn't noticed, there are no datable girls on the island. You will probably want a date after a while."

"I had planned to invite a friend down for a trial stay. If I'm lucky, she might like it."

"Sounds like a plan. Come on up to the club tonight, and we can talk about your plan over a beer."

Jack was a self-made pilot from Vermont. His niche was as engineer and pilot for the Coles. His worksite was a sheet-metal building full of golf carts, welders, and compressors and all the parts and tools necessary to keep a complicated airplane in the air. He could fix anything, or as Jack put it, weld tin to a turnip. His optimism and mechanical knowledge were impressive; his skepticism about our place on an island being developed for profit was obvious. He was open to new ideas, and that was good enough for me.

There is something magical about walking barefoot in the sand on a dark path after sunset. The tropical bushes hung over the edge of the golf cart path to trace your way. All the lizards and iguanas had found a warm spot for the night. Even the Caribbean nighthawk had stopped buzzing and found a dwarf yellow pine to stick to for the night. The sand was still warm between the toes, and the breeze had cooled to a slight chill. In the blazing sun of twenty-three degrees north latitude, seventy degrees was chilly. Far down the path the lights of the Meridian Club beckoned to me. When I walked into the bar, everyone turned to look. I pointed to a St. Pauli Girl; Earl, the bartender, smiled and set one on the bar.

"We can't get milk or peanut butter or bagels, but the bar has fifteen different kinds of beer," said Jack. "How was your first week in paradise?"

"Everything is great," I said. "There do not seem to be many young women on the island. I thought since there was a hotel here, there would be some unattached girls to talk to."

"Nope," said Jack, "the crowd that comes here are either young couples with no kids or grandparents with the grandchildren, newlyweds, or nearly dead. The last thirty-year-old woman here was on vacation from her kids and husband for a little hanky-panky. There are certainly a lot of possibilities with that scenario."

"I'm planning to bring my friend down from Virginia," I said. "She is a linguist and a teacher. I thought she could help some of the native guys with English, using the dive manual as a textbook."

"Well," Jack said, "that sounds like a good idea. I was worried that my girlfriend would need someone her age to socialize with, and this may be a good thing. Stevie came down last year for a while and complained that she could only go to the beach and sunbathe so much."

It took a while to arrange communication with Frankie and Stevie without phones or consistent mail service. A trip to Provo would solve all these problems, so Jack and I flew over the next day to put our letters directly in the hands of an outgoing tourist. We went to the grocery store for ice cream and a few supplies. The store had very little variety, with prices higher than the sky. Cuba was the only place I had been with less food and higher prices. At least you could get vegetables and fruits in Cuba. The Caicos were so dry that corn and tomatoes were the only crop, and that was just a backyard thing. A vegetarian nightmare, all our crops came in cans.

We gathered up an armload of green beans and Beanie Weenies, all in cans, and boxes of Kraft Cheese dinners.

We flew out over the boat harbor on the north end of Provo, heading back to Pine Cay. Jack told me the resort and marina below us was Leeward Going Through. I noticed a large ketch lying close in toward the mangroves. *Why would anyone leave a nice boat like that so close to the shore?* I thought.

Life now consisted of feeding conch, building an addition onto the dome, spear-fishing for lunch and dinner, underwater slideshows in the evening at the club, and working with the local guys and teaching them scuba and to speak and write the queen's/president's English

Chuck announced one night that it was time to fly up to Miami to meet with folks from a nonprofit grant organization. We were in the business of seeking donated money, and Chuck was the main glad hand for the foundation. The nonprofit was called the Foundation for PRIDE. The acronym meant preserve reefs and islands from development and exploitation. The natives liked the pride part, and the rest of it probably aggravated the greed heads. Kathy and I said goodbye to Chuck as he boarded the ubiquitous Otter commuter to Provo. It was always a fingers-crossed moment as the Otter pulled up hard to avoid the skyward pointing tail of the last Cherokee 6 that had nosed into the mangroves. That plane hit the bushes because the pilot's dog was resting his foot on the fuel shutoff valve. They don't fly long without fuel.

My job was not to worry about loosening the purse strings of potential donors but to get ready for a college group from the Midwest. John Iverson, a former island resident/graduate student, had secured a PhD from the University of Florida and a job at Earlham College in Indiana as far away from his study species as he could get. This was not intentional. Biology teaching positions are not a dime a dozen, especially if your field of study is herpetology. Pine and Little Water Cay were blessed with rock iguanas. John was bringing his students down to Pine Cay on the college winter break to introduce them to an iguana or two and study tropical biology. He also missed the Beanie Weenies and Kraft Cheese Dinners he reportedly lived on as a student.

John and I snorkeled them, dragged them through mangrove swamps, regaled them with folk music, taught them how to catch birds and swat mosquitoes. The meals were much like his college days with a lobster feast thrown in for good measure.

This sortie into contract education was our foundation's first experience in making money the old-fashioned way—working for it. Any teaching program requires a compressed amount of effort. Pulling all this information together and redistributing it with a little in situ experience was most gratifying. We were all excited by this experience. Chuck was looking for more opportunities like the Earlham group to reach out to.

It was winter vacation time, and tourists were filling the hotel rooms looking for something exciting to do. Chuck and I decided to offer a smidgen of reef ecology, snorkeling in the subject, and an underwater photography course for tourists. Talk about a great hit. I was soon up to my hips in fawning tourists wanting the Cousteau experience. Vacant niches are few and far between on this planet, and we had blindly settled into a new one, one that no one would even care about for another ten years. Not a wasted ten years. Just think of all the burgers that were flipped and all the tables waited on by marginally employed biology majors until they finally became employed in ecotourism.

The drill was to have a slideshow the first evening of a tourist group arrival extolling the beauty of the nearly virgin barrier reef. Then I would do a little impromptu guitar-accompanied folk singing and then let them know about our tax-deductible course in reef ecology and underwater photography.

This course kept everyone busy in paradise learning about the nuts and bolts of tropical reefs while also learning how to shoot and develop underwater slides. The prices were reasonable, and the classes were full. We had cornered the ecological education market at a time when 99.9 percent of humanity didn't even know what an ecology market was. We didn't care; the market was ours, and we were on a roll, regardless of the rest of humanity's ignorance.

Underwater snorkel safaris, evenings in the darkroom developing film with the student photographers, and evening slideshows at the club cemented our relationship with the island's owners and managers. Chuck and Bill's plan was coming together to have a vacation spot and, perhaps, an expensive piece of paradise to purchase, with lots of environmental conscience as part of the planning.

Dealing with the struggles of day-to-day living got all of us up early in the morning and late to bed. The only thing missing for Jack and me was female companionship. My friend Frankie arrived first. She came in on the biweekly commuter plane. I moved her into the just-finished wing of the geodesic dome. I had been working evenings with one of the local carpenters to fashion a kitchen/sleeping quarters from a twenty-five-by-twelve-foot wing of the dome. We used hand tools to saw around corners and trim them with hand-sawn veneer. I was working with a direct descendent of Africans that were captured and sold by their brothers to white slavers and packed like lumber aboard a leaky old wooden ship. Who knows how many survived and what race they were. All that history is now sawing lumber, laying bricks, singing, fishing, and laughing in a land they unintentionally ran aground on.

Frankie and I had been introduced to each other by a mutual friend while I was in New Jersey taking a course in aerial remote sensing. We were both unattached, free spirits, and liked adventure. She came for a vacation, but I hoped she would stay. Her first impression of our living space was to call it the fishbowl. It had a pair of sliding glass doors on one end of the room looking out over the low vegetation and right down the path to the club. There were no curtain stores, so a sheet had to suffice. We also shared the shower, the head, toilet, and the acoustics with anyone inside the dome. Privacy was a bit of an issue, but who needs privacy when you are living in paradise? Yes, that did wear thin almost immediately, but what did I know at age thirty-three. If men were born with this kind of information, they would not be called men. It takes time; the more evolved you are, the less time maturity takes. Personal evolution is not my strong suit, and it took a while. We eventually moved into a vacant home while the owners were off the island.

Stevie arrived at about the same time as Frankie. We now officially had a group of men paired off with a group of women, or three couples. Unlike a commune, we were all there for different reasons. Suffice it to say, sun and fun were a common thread. At this point, I had not read *Fatu Hiva* by Thor Heyerdahl, *The Island* by Aldous Huxley, or *The Mosquito Coast* by Paul Theroux. Each one of these novels extolled the problems with educated, well-intentioned, idealistic young expatriates interfacing with native cultures, and conservative entrenched expatriates. Heyerdahl and his wife found the local Polynesians welcoming, but the local Catholic priest was fearful of losing his position with the natives. This (island paranoia) caused the priest to put out a hit on the young well-educated couple from Norway. They were only there to study plant migration. The priest, tortured by isolation and feelings of grandeur, could find no other option but to kill his imagined rivals. Fortunately, Thor and his wife managed to escape the island after hiding in a shelter cave for a month. So much for paradise.

The characters in the *Mosquito Coast* had a priest with a gun. Jesus never envisioned a shepherd with a gun. The same paranoia was at work. The Huxley novel was introspection on a utopian island with no harbor, next to an island with a good harbor and a military government set on developing its neighbor. The Utopians never had a chance.

We did not have a priest on Pine Cay, but we did have an island manager. Nick was a pragmatist in his 24-7 job to keep the generators running, supplying the power for all the energy-hungry appliances from a far-off civilization transplanted to an island with no resources except wind and sun. His boss wanted him to make it work like the States. We were preaching a renaissance in thinking about wind and solar power that few forward-thinkers would accept for at least a generation. Nick and Paul were exhibiting all the symptoms of (island paranoia). The rest of us had a slightly different mindset. Jack, Stevie, Frankie, and I were there for the adventure. The rest had a portion of their ego attached to their jobs. Once your ego becomes attached to a niche, the territorial imperative kicks in, and you are anchored by your hypothalamus to the situation or substrate you're on.

A Wonderful Christmas Present

The day before Christmas, we were informed by a tourist that she had seen a pod of dolphins stranded on a narrow beach south of the Meridian Club. I grabbed a pug, an all-terrain vehicle, recruited a student intern, and headed for the stranding beach. We found eighteen large dark-gray dolphins stranded on the back side of a filled-in pass. The water was very shallow with a gradually sloping beach. Three of the animals were already dead, and ten were beached and sunburned. A few were in the water, on their sides, with blowholes in and out of the water. The two that were still mobile were doing their best to save their companions by rolling them over on their stomachs, preventing them from drowning. Moving these large animals was not an option with just two of us. We splashed water on the ones near the shore and headed back to get the Boston Whaler and an old inflatable for dolphin transport. I figured that we could save one by deflating the rubber boat and floating it back to the lab. The tide was up enough to get us across the flats and onto the stranding beach. It took only thirty minutes to get there with the boat on a plane. We towed the inflatable behind us.

When we arrived, the dolphins, high on the beach, were dead, but we still had seven in relatively good shape. The first job was to deflate the rubber boat and slide the healthiest dolphin aboard. We lifted its head into the boat and worked our way back to the tail. We struggled, but we did manage to accomplish the job in short order. As the afternoon was waning, we were trying to tow a six-hundred-pound dolphin in a partially inflated rubber boat, across a rapidly swallowing grass flat, with a boat that drew too much water. Our only choice was to get out and push. The rescue had changed flavor. We were now pushing several thousand pounds of animal, fiberglass boat, and assorted boat gear through very shallow water in our bare feet. The turtle grass and soft sand gobbled up our steps as we trudged along through the dark. Stingrays are frequent visitors to the grass flats, especially at night. I could not help but think about the possible intersection with one of those especially large foraging rays. A big ray can sport a four-foot stinger with hundreds of barbs, all fixed like an unyielding arrowhead. The bankside of Pine Cay was uninhabited, leaving it invisible in the dark. Without lights on the island, we had only the stars to navigate by. Since the island lay north to south, the polestar was our beacon. I knew the water would get deeper when we reached the inlet leading to the lab, so we pushed on.

The turtle grass is partnered with calcium-secreting algae that are sharp enough to puncture our bare feet. This calcium eventually builds up, as the plant dies, to form wonderfully soft white Caribbean beaches. In its raw form, it is sharp and painful to uncovered feet. We were cold, tired, and temporarily lost. It was time to climb into the whaler and wait for the tide. At first light, we had enough water under us to use the motor again. Now that we could see the lab, we found our way to the deep-water channel and back to the dock. The big female dolphin was released in the boat basin by deflating the rubber boat. She seemed okay for the time.

We headed back to the club to recruit the breakfast crowd for a Christmas rescue. Armed with two pugs with trailers and ten people and a big rug, we set out to haul the remaining dolphins to the ocean side of the beach and freedom. Everyone was enthusiastic and pitched in with zeal. Six of us lifted each dolphin onto the rug, which allowed us to lift them high enough to set them gently into the utility trailer. A short trip across the beach, by pug, led the Christmas tourists and dolphins to deeper cooler water. The first to make the journey was an adult female caretaker dolphin, perhaps the matriarch of the pod/clan. She was still moving among her less-healthy companions, making sure blowholes were vertical and splashing them with water. The reasoning was that she would attract/beckon the rest of the survivors out into safe water.

Six of us hefted her off the trailer, down the beach, and slowly into the water. The water temperature was cooler to the touch than the shallow tropical-sun-heated water on the bank. This temperature difference must have given her a boost. She swam offshore for a thousand feet and stopped. A minute passed, and she disappeared. I stood waist-deep, straining to see a fin, but nothing. Everyone was a bit disappointed by the outcome. Had our matriarch become selfish and uninterested in the future of her family? It was a bit disappointing until I felt a big bump on my side. Fortunately, it was the big female dolphin and not a member of a long list of things I didn't want bumping me in waist-deep water. A cheer went up on the beach behind me, and the pug roared to life for the next trip. We scrambled back and forth across the beach six more times. Caretaker dolphin moved back offshore to beckon each new arrival out to her position. Within an hour, we had transported four healthy dolphins and two that were less healthy. We took turns swimming with them until they acclimated themselves to the new temperature and surroundings.

I later identified the stranded dolphins as rough-toothed dolphins. They spend their life in deep ocean, far from shore and human contact. We were probably the first humans these beautiful little whales had ever seen. I hope we left them with a good impression of humankind. I do know that the winter visitors to our little island had an experience they will treasure the rest of their lives. Seldom do we get to touch the wild, and even less seldom does it touch back. When we arrived back at the boat basin next to the lab, we were sad to find the dolphin we had spent all night rescuing had died. The fourteen-year-old native girl who had been working next to me for twenty hours, attempting to rescue a pod of dolphins, asked me if we were going to eat the dead female dolphin. The question stunned me, but I recovered enough to tell her that it was not culturally acceptable to eat dolphins. I was well aware that hunter/gatherers in third-world countries eat dolphins all the time.

We unceremoniously towed her out to sea and released her to the deep. She sank straight down into twelve thousand feet of water, and it was over. A prominent New England family later helped the young island girl go to a private school in the States. I hope she did well there. She could run like the wind. She was certainly sport-scholarship material.

OUR ELECTRONS ARE BETTER
THAN YOUR ELECTRONS

Now that all the potential seats at the table were filled, it was time to have weekly planning sessions. Bill, the owner of the island, and Chuck spent more time ruminating on the course Pine Cay would be sailing from week to week. Paul, Nick, and I were the ground people, ready to act on any new ideas brought to the table each week. The planning sessions dealt with building-lot size, power and water needs, supply status, and how PRIDE was going to interface with the profit end of the island. Our job was to provide dive education, environmental awareness, and underwater photography lessons. We also offered underwater slideshows, tours of the conch research facility, and some immersion into alternate energy.

The bone of contention was always the subject of power. Tourists in the '70s were not "green." Nobody cared about the price of fuel or greenhouse gasses. Cold beer, hot showers, and regular meals in front of a great beach were all that mattered. As long as Nick kept at least one of the two generators running, anything was possible. The time, parts, fuel, noise, and general aggravation of running a small power source based on the gas/diesel era was wearing heavily on Nick. When things went bad in the generator shed, Nick was there. He was also in charge of water coming out of the ground and sewage going into the ground.

We had endless discussions on water-conserving toilets, reduced-flow showerheads, recycling gray water, and composting. It all made sense to Chuck and me and little or no sense to them. It meant changing the infrastructure of the present and doing the ostrich thing for the future. Of course, Bill was writing us a whopping big check every year to "just be free and creative." It really does relieve one of many burdens to be free of the profit motive. "Grant us all grants" is the mantra of all research scientists. Total up the supplies, transportation, and time and present the bill. Some caring capitalist usually writes the check. That's the way it works. My job was to sell our services to the client/tourists and begin to self-support our research and education. This role placed me in the netherworld between the idealists and the pragmatists. My presence there and the straddling act I appeared to be doing attracted the ever-curious developer type to my corner of the bar in the evening.

"What's that Chuck guy up to anyway?" would be their first approach. They would buy me a drink and hope for a revelation. Conservation of resources and sequestering of parkland (habitat) were not in the average Realtor's vocabulary. Land is for developing, and anybody not doing that is suspicious at best and criminal at worst. The best I could do at that point was shrug and change the subject.

It did seem that Chuck had garnered a reputation for being in favor of limiting development. Why raise the antidevelopment dust in such a small world? The expatriate world was immediate. Nothing was said or done on the island without light speed knowledge to all interested parties, and all were interested. Once my toe was in the pool, the ripples spread to all corners. I was the arbitrator or explainer to an argument that is still going on. I once read a statement, supposedly channeled from the universe, to a carpenter, laying back in his BarcaLounger, and written down by his wife. "Ecology before economy and education before everything." I believe it, but I'm not sure it will ever happen. It will never happen if we don't talk about it, so I talked about it.

Being a live-and-let-live kind of guy, I was striving to keep my tent somewhere between the established (developer/nondeveloper) camps on the island. Alternate energy was considered a bold statement against heavy development. Our electrons were weak and shortsighted. High voltage, high-watt energy was the mantra. Selling lots and building houses was a logistical nightmare to start with. Building solar water heaters and incorporating solar voltaics and wind generators was not on the table. Civilization had grabbed hold of "live better electrically" and left the woodburning, kerosene, and Florida solar hot-water heater—even propane—culture behind. The natives were still using the old-fashioned technology, along with Coleman fuel cookstoves. We were trying to educate the locals about alternate energy before they took the diesel electric road, but the tide had already turned.

We had started a workshop in the evenings to train some of the local guys how to maintain and repair wind generators. These units were built in Wisconsin back in the 1930s. They had worked well for rural Midwestern farms. Parts were still available from a company in Nebraska and a small shop in Miami. Without the Internet and regular jet transport, all the parts for anything usually required a trip to Miami. Once we had parts, we put our students to work rebuilding the very simple old wind generators. Before long, our team of local students had rebuilt the generators and constructed a tower to mount the first unit. We had a small ceremony while placing the generator on its thirty-foot high perch. Batteries had arrived aboard a fifty-four-foot sailing yacht, along with two electric golf carts. The plan was to replace the gas-sucking, ear-splitting pugs with silent electric golf carts that could be charged from the alternating current (AC) at the club or the direct current (DC) at our radical end of the island. The golf carts did not care about politics, just electrons.

The new twenty-five amp-hour wind generator provided more than enough power to run the fluorescent lights, electric typewriters, and water pump. One of our daily routines was refueling the kerosene refrigerators. The job required pulling the two-gallon fuel tank out from under the refrigeration unit and filling the container with kerosene. The wick on the fuel tank was made of silk. After the user put a match to the silk, it becomes extremely delicate. The long trip from the refinery to the island, coupled with condensation in the fuel barrel and a rich warm environment for fungus to grow, provides a less-than-usable fuel to power a refrigerator or anything else requiring clean fresh fuel. The dirty carbon-covered wicks always broke during refueling, making the job messy and unpleasant. This, coupled with the frequency requirements of once-per-week refills, led us to think about electrical refrigeration.

Several of the storage batteries had already blown their tops off due to too much electricity and not enough usages. We were in the enviable position of trying to use our excess electrical power. Electrical refrigeration was the answer. Like the golf cart, the refrigerator does not care where the electrons come from as long as they keep coming. Our 1930's vintage wind generators merrily cranked out an average 10 amps per hour for twelve to fourteen hours a day. The math is so easy even I can figure 120–140 amp hours of production daily. The fridge pulled about 90 amps per day. The lights, stereo, typewriters, and water pumps used about 20 amps per day. That is a total of 110 amp-hours of DC electricity every day. We were always close to our production, except the days when the wind did not blow. The trick was to capture the excess power on the windy days to get us through the calm days. This, of course, required great numbers of storage batteries. Sears was not around the corner, so batteries were constantly being brought from Miami to replace worn-out ones.

Nothing is free and certainly not when it comes to the first-world technology of battery production. Our daily usage called for all our single generator could produce. Golf carts had four 220-amp-hour six-volt batteries, totaling 440 amps of storage at twelve volts. A golf cart can use 100 amps in two hours of usage, which would, by my reckoning, require another wind generator just to keep up with that transportation cost. Our interim solution was to hook up to the diesel power grid until we could put more alternate energy online.

I later mounted the same wind generator to the mizzenmast of my sailboat, *Fortunella*, to produce power for the same group of reasons as I had done on the island. When the wind was blowing hard, and the amp meter was bumping twenty-five amps, we could run the vacuum cleaner and the blender. This would clean the boat and produce a great margarita, all with the power of the wind. Solar-powered margaritas are so much better than nuclear, oil, gas, or water-powered margaritas. In 1979, solar power was just a science experiment. To extract 2 watts of DC power out of a square foot of solar voltaic material was difficult, even with all the sun we had. By 1990, that same square foot produced 13.75 watts, which is more than an amp hour of DC power.

After dinner at the club, the conversation ranged from what kind of electrons did we drive up to the club on, to how little water does that limited flush toilet you guys have actually use? People are always suspicious of change, and the word *limited* is a word only a Communist would dare utter. When you are on the frontier, conservation is not the mantra, even if there is very little water or electricity.

OUR FIRST GIG

Kathy and Chuck are self-starters. That is a prerequisite for anyone living on a small island with a desire to modify their surroundings. Building a home or a research facility out of tropical scrub and providing some comforts of civilization require a fresh energized start for each day. To keep yourself from veering off course and going to the beach, you have to stay focused. *Focus* was the watchword for almost everything we did. I received my marching orders from Chuck the first working day I was there.

After Christmas, I would host a twenty-day minicourse in marine biology for Earlham College. I would be responsible for all the logistics of this field course in tropical biology. The second order of business was teaching a course in underwater photography and reef ecology. This was aimed at the few tourists that were coming to the Meridian Club. The hope was that it would provide income for the foundation and a lot of goodwill for the developer. Chuck and Kathy would have a slideshow at the club once a week to let people see the unspoiled reef and all the critters and flora. It was unusual, at that time, to go to a tropical destination and find a staff of marine biologists offering scuba lessons and courses in ecology and UW photography. We had no idea we were the vanguard of the ecotourism movement.

I studied recent scientific articles on zooxanthellic algae, which live in the outer membrane of coral polyps. This, at the time, was the beginning of understanding how coral made a living in relatively sterile ocean water. The coral membrane was a good habitat for a single-celled plant that was busy photosynthesizing sugars and starches. The alga, a primary producer, was being raised and eaten by the coral, a primary consumer. The coral was then being eaten by the rest of the coral-munching fish and invertebrates on the reef and creating a food base for all the other swimming and crawling creatures in the reef community. With this understanding and a Nikonos underwater camera, students could be introduced to a world that was alien to most of them and go back to their regular lives with a new and better understanding of an ocean community.

I realized a coral community was just like a human city with its surrounding agricultural areas. A coral reef is an isolated group of reef-building animals that constantly sequesters natural resources like calcium (Ca) and carbon dioxide (CO_2) and build massive skeletons made of calcium carbonate. These reefs were surrounded by grass flats that support large numbers of grazing animals, such as conch and echinoderms (starfish and urchins). Fish and crabs and lobsters are constantly breaking down the reef by consuming the coral. The excrement from all these critters is mixed with ground-up coral or beach sand. This sand migrates away from the reef to form the substrate that makes up the grass flats. Coralline alga, which grows on the grass flats, also forms a calcium crust on the grass leaves. This slowly falls off and contributes to the calcareous substrate.

This scenario can be compared to human endeavor around any population center. People or lobsters are all just trying to build a life, and in the process, something else is broken down. Humans quarry limestone to make concrete for buildings. The limestone is nothing more than ancient coral, and the surrounding sand flats, now pushed thousands of feet in the air by plate tectonics. We are using the same calcium to make our homes that the coral extracted from the sea, to make its home, millions of years ago. And the beat goes on.

Planet Earth started out as a life-size chunk of the periodic chart. All the elements are combined, then recombined over 14.5 billion years and continually recycled into new forms inorganically, then taken by living plants and animals and reformed again. The organic remains of all that biological activity is now stored as fossil fuel. Two hundred and fifty million years of stored photosynthetic energy stored in coal, oil, and natural gas. Our ancestors managed to get along for several hundred thousand years just burning trees to cook and keep warm. Their transport was by foot, boat, and horse.

The invention of the steam engine gave humanity a mechanical power source fired by organically formed fuel. One hundred and fifty years later, we have used up half of the resources generated since the Carboniferous Period 250 million years ago.

I took the flattop to Provo to pick up the students who were landing in the afternoon. There, on the edge of the deep water, sat the ketch I had seen when Jack and I had flown over the harbor a month ago. A slow pass revealed a European-style forty-foot sailing vessel with weathered teak decks, broken stanchions, hatches open, and uncovered sails. The ports were duct-taped on the inside, like a military vessel during a war. My guess was that the drug smugglers

did not want to be seen at night. The boat looked like a great lady that had been treated poorly. This was a yacht of substance. I could see a brass plate with the builder's name and place of construction to the left of the aft companionway. A proud builder left his mark.

Pressed for time, I pushed the clutch forward and throttled up toward the dock. I backed down and slid to starboard into a huge grader tire on the outside of the seawall.

"Hey, Joyce, do you know anything about the ketch that looks like a ghost ship?" I asked.

"It was left here six months ago by a bunch of guys from Miami. They left me $75 to sweep up the pot seeds and keep an eye on it," she said.

"So it's a smuggler." She shrugged and invited me in for a cold drink.

The students were packed into a small bus with lots of luggage and spare food. When you fly from Indiana, in January, to the tropics, you do not arrive with a tan. The Midwestern students were as white as white people get without the stimulus of photons on melanin. They were about to be stimulated by photons coming in at a disturbingly high angle. After introductions, I explained the dangers of the tropical sun so they might have a chance of avoiding severe sunburn or, worse, sun poisoning. Mosquitos, scorpions, stingrays, and sharks all hang in the tropics, but sunburn will put you out of action quick. Everybody greased up, and off we went.

We spent the next eighteen days snorkeling on the grass flats, in the mangroves, and on the barrier reefs on the northwest corner of the Caicos Bank. In this third-world country, all the aquatic habitats were untouched by the industrial age. The local fishermen still traveled in thirty-foot hand-hewn planked wooden boats. They would sail out to the fishing/conching grounds, anchor, and send the crew out in small dinghy boats powered with a sculling oar. You cannot rape a resource when your average speed is three knots. In those days, when outboard motors were uncommon, the captain and crew were unfettered by the stress of mechanical maintenance concerns. There are always enough things to do on a fishing boat to keep you busy without having to deal with a gas-powered devil, built in a far-off land with no local parts to repair them.

I hold in my heart the joy of these fishermen as they sailed out onto the Caicos Bank, four or five men in ragged shorts and tattered T-shirts, bare feet on a wood deck, feeling the pull of the trades on the great mainsail. Fishing trips planned around weather forecasts by the experience of the seasoned captain. No weather channel, just the weather eye of a dark-skin man, feeling the wind on his face and the trace of high stratus clouds streaming in from the north, heralding a future north wind to bring him home. Between the southeast trades and clockwise turn of the winter-wind cycle, the men will gain the conch patch, anchor up the mother vessel, and scull the dinghy boats out onto the bank with nothing but a wooden view bucket, a pole with a rebar hook fastened to one end, and a stick of sugarcane to chew on.

The afternoon clouds, tracing shadows across the turtle grass, mark their day. The clouds momentarily darken the view into the gin-clear water. The man waits for the sun, spots the sharp spire of the mature conch in a patch of grass, and lowers his pole. The hook is pushed into the soft sand bottom, rotated under the lip of the shell, and skillfully lifted toward the boat gunnel. The snail is dropped to the floor, and the man moves on. He keeps sculling until the boat is full.

The afternoon wind is up, and the conch-laden wooden skiffs are unable to scull too windward. The boat captain has already retrieved the anchor and hoisted the jib. He falls off, eases the jib, and sails to leeward of his small fleet of dinghy boats and reanchors the mother boat. The dinghy boats pay off and, with the wind at their backs, unite and off-load their catch. They knock a hole in the lip of the shells and string the whole catch together and leave them in the water under the boat until they retrieve them for the return trip. Without ice, the conch would spoil in the tropical heat. Corralled on the bottom by a long length of rope through their common shells, they will stay alive and fresh for the homeward journey. The gods have choreographed this dance with the wind and waves, conch and wood. I once asked a man why he fished this way, and he grinned as he leaned back against his wooden mast, wiggled his bare feet, and said, "I like to keep me toes free." All this man's effort was directed toward free toes. The image of his big horny brown toes, moving freely in the warm humid air, remains etched in my memory.

By the fifteenth day, the students were well-tanned and accustomed to the prickly nature of the environment. They all had a course in underwater photography, had learned to snorkel on a pristine barrier reef, and sampled the lizard and bird population. I had taken a shine to a wholesome young coed. Chuck and Kathy had left the island for a short trip to Miami, so I invited the coed over to their place since their couch was my bunk at that time. I was young, and so was she, so we did what young healthy people do when they find themselves in paradise. It was not meant to be permanent; we made no promises. We had a nice time, interrupted only by the unexpected return of Kathy. She was surprised to find us on the couch but made no judgment.

On the twentieth day, the student's time on the island was over, and the whole group was ferried back to Provo for the flight back to the States. I bid goodbye to my new friend and settled down for the coming tourist season. The plan was to offer minicourses in reef ecology, underwater photography, and an occasional dive certification class. My friend Frankie, from Alexandria, Virginia, had written me a letter with a desire to visit the island. She was a person of many talents and had knitted together a tangle of teaching positions in the DC area. None of these jobs were offering career tracks or offered benefits for that matter. She was ready for adventure, and we were both looking forward to getting back together.

FRANKIE AND STEVIE WERE LOVERS

Stevie and Frankie were Jack's and my girlfriends. What were the odds of Jack and I having girlfriends with guys' names like that? Considering the lay of the land and the scarcity of young, single, attractive women, we were fairly excited. The downside to small third-world islands is that the women that visit are usually newlyweds or nearly deads. Importing dates seemed to be a good option; our dates were probably as excited as we were to be traveling to an exotic destination with free room and adventure.

The geodesic dome, all three stories, was mostly finished by the time the girls arrived. After the student course, I set to work with a local carpenter named Ernie to finish off one of the wings for my apartment. While we were finishing off the kitchen counter, I remarked to Ernie that it would be nice to trim the edge of the plywood counter with a piece of veneer. He immediately walked over, picked up a two-by-four and a handsaw, and proceeded to slice a thin ribbon of wood off the length of the board. That small act changed my life. I was no longer hobbled by civilization. I could, with a knife, a handsaw, and a roll of duct tape, build or do anything.

Our daily activities started at sunrise, with homemade sweet bread from the construction crew's cook. Peanut butter and jelly from the store in Provo, and an occasional egg, if the chickens were ambitious enough to lay. We were structured by Chuck and Aldus Huxley in *Brave New World* to perform our required duties toward a philosophical end. None of us were there for money or praise. Some were there for adventure, and others had a plan. Chuck's Annapolis education was overriding his sense of adventure. Jack was there to mess with airplanes and, perhaps, own one in time. Kathy was part of Chuck's thing and to further her understanding of conch and all the other biological wonders of the tropical surroundings. Frankie and Stevie were there out of curiosity and adventure. And I, like Jack, was there for the experience and the possibility of getting, in my case, a boat.

After breakfast, the paid staff, Chuck, Kathy and I, would have a short meeting to plan the day and then start to work.

The conch table sand had to be shoveled back into the ocean and all-new sand put in. Conch and cats do not like poop in their sand. We then went out on the bank in a Boston Whaler to collect new clean fresh algae for the conch to graze on. While we were out there, we would try to locate the tagged wild conch that were in Kathy's ranging study. She had placed a yellow floating tag on a group of conch so they were easy to spot by us and a whole host of critters and people. It is hard enough to convince a local fisherman not to take a study conch. It was impossible to convince a spotted eagle ray or a nurse shark that the tagged conch had scientific significance. Studying snail movements in the open ocean is a frustrating process.

We would return with a boatload of macroalgae (algae big enough to see) and the attached microalgae that the conch would eat. At that time, it was not evident what part of the boatload of green stuff they ate. We only knew they spent a lot of time with their mouthparts, sucking on big algae. The whole thing was labor-intensive and fun. Lunchtime was a break for more sweet bread and something out of a can, unless there was fresh protein leftover from the night before. This was where things got different.

After lunch, I would dive into the cut with snorkel gear and a Bahamian sling. The sling was a six-foot stainless steel shaft with a barbed tip. It was launched through a round block of wood with surgical tubing lashed to the back end. There were a lot of misses, to begin with, and a free-flying spear shaft is not easy to find if you are not paying attention. Best to shoot into the bank for easy retrieval. I eventually recalled my archery training as a youth in Japan. My master told me to "become the arrow." Zen spearfishing is an art that takes time and practice. I had the time and the motivation; success meant dinner from nature, not a can.

Frankie was genetically predisposed to learning languages and conversed with the speakers of those languages as easily as she learns how those people cooked and ate her food. She was genetically predisposed to cooking great meals, and I did my best to provide her with a great variety of seafood to challenge her. Lobster, conch, grouper, snapper, triggerfish, it was all rich and wonderful and made us yearn for hot dogs. I know that sounds crazy, but sometimes processed meat or canned veggies are all it takes.

We would eat at least one meal at the club each week when the tourists arrived. After the meal, one of us would put on a slideshow with aerial photos of the island and lots of underwater pictures of the local residents on the reef. We would regale the crowd with life histories of many of the sea creatures and then offer to take them on an underwater safari, with tanks or snorkels, and rent them waterproof cameras. After the trip was over, we would show them how to develop the slide film. If that weren't enough, I would get up and sing folk songs and a little Broadway stuff before we started taking reservations for the next day. Ecotourism was born.

The winter season was moving along with warm days and cool nights. All the residents on our north end of the island were paired up and into a daily routine. Chuck and Kathy were finishing their house and generally well entrenched in their daily routine. Jack was busy keeping a myriad of golf carts and airplanes running. Stevie spent her time at the club swimming in the pool, playing tennis, and keeping Jack company. Frankie decided to take a stab at teaching reading and writing to some of the local guys working for the foundation. Raymond and Dolphus both wanted to get their dive certification cards. They were like fish in the water but not so good at bookwork. I would teach from the book in the evenings, and Frankie would help them do their homework from the dive book. They were motivated to learn to dive and read, and Frankie was a great teacher.

Both Frankie and I were well accepted by the locals. We spent many nights playing the guitar and learning the local dance steps. Reggae was moving up through the islands. A "jump up" was a local music-and-dance event. The guitars were strung with different-size monofilament fishing line. A bucket, with a goatskin stretched over it, was the rhythm section. There were washboards, washtubs, and conch horns to fill out the string and horn sections. It was all great fun and a great release from the stress of saving the planet. It's hard to believe, but the constant tug of war between Chuck and Nick and Bill Coles, and now me, was getting on all our nerves.

At this point, all the characters in the play were on board. Like a pack of wolves, or a pride of lions, the individuals were looking for their places in the hierarchy; island paranoia was in full bloom.

AND DARKNESS FELL

The local government was located in Grand Turk. The leaders were very happy to have a nonprofit working on a fisheries problem and teaching a summer-school course in marine science. With his diplomacy and optimism, Chuck had smoothed the waters for work permits and a whole host of other problems. He was a can-do kinda guy, and people could see that right away. He was so good at his job a politico in Grand Turk donated a wonderful twenty-one-foot Drascombe Lugger to the foundation. This wonderful little English-built open sailboat was yawl-rigged and equipped with a British Seagull outboard motor. Frankie and I had been eyeing this little beauty for a while. We decided to sail over to Provo for the day and pick up some groceries and an ice cream cone. It seemed very doable.

We had to assemble some serious brawn to push the sailboat off the beach. Fortunately, the construction crew was on the island, so all, with a great deal of frivolity, pulled her down to the water. Extra water, some bread and peanut butter, and we were on our way. The passes between the islands were scoured deep with the tide passing in and out. We tacked furiously for forty minutes to clear the end of the island and gain the shallow clear water of the bank. Once in open water, we could make for Provo with the hope that the tide was fair in Leeward Going Through. Nothing is better than surging along in a stout little boat under a full press of sail. She steered nicely and could slide over all the grass beds and small coral heads by simply lifting the centerboard for a moment and kicking up the rudder. We were reaching, so I had no concern about returning on a foul wind or tide. We were swept into the cut and moved so fast with the tide we barely made the dock. We gibed over quickly to gain the dock but could not maintain enough headway against the tide. An enormous black fella rushed to our aid by tossing a line to Frankie and hauling us up short to the big tire on the seawall.

"Thanks, man," I said to our savior.

"That's no problem. It happens all the time. You folks stayin' for lunch?" This man's manner won me over immediately. His head was as broad as his smile.

"Who's the cook?" I asked.

"That's me, mon."

We were friends for life, and I knew instantly, it just happens that way. One minute, you're strangers, and the next moment, you have known each other for a lifetime, or maybe more.

Calvin, the cook, helped us both onto the dock and let us know lunch was triggerfish, with peas and rice. The dressing on the salad, if there was one, would be Thousand Island. It was always Thousand Island, not Russian or anything else, Thousand Island; it matched the geology. Calvin was all about who we were and what we were doing.

The sailboat was still in the harbor, so I asked, "What's the deal with the ketch out there?"

"Some druggies left it here about a month or so back. It happens all the time."

"Do you think it belongs to them or someone else?" I asked.

"They looked and talked like they were from New York, certainly not Belgium. They ate and drank a lot, generally treated everyone poorly, and left in a hurry. Said something about motor problems."

"Who do you have there, Calvin?" We all turned to greet a middle-aged woman standing outside the circular restaurant.

"This is Ron and Frankie from Pine Cay. They come here to shop in town. Are you going that way?" Calvin said.

"The suburban will leave in about an hour. My name is Joyce."

"That would be great," I said. "Is there any way we can get out to see that boat over there by the mangroves?"

"Ya sure, the Rasta guy is gone, and no telling what it's like down below after that fella," said Joyce.

Joyce, Frankie, and I climbed into the yawl, and I fired up the Seagull to motor across the cut to the boat. She, the boat, was not a pretty sight. The decks were weathered badly, all the hatches were open, and the mainsail hung off the boom in the scorching sunlight. No covers on anything except the cockpit. The dodger was weathered but intact. There were knife marks on the aft deck right next to the cockpit. My guess, they were cleaning fish or cutting bait on the teak deck. This was offensive to me in so many ways but probably never occurred to the Neanderthal doing the cutting. Teak decks are the last bit of frosting put on a wealthy man's boat. The old-world tropical hardwood screwed and glued down with infinite care by a trained marine carpenter with considerable time on the job and much knee damage. The interior was equally neglected and abused. The varnish near the companionways was stripped by the sun and replaced by oil and dirt from many hands and shoulders passing in and out. The once-gleaming teak and holly cabin sole now resembled an old weathered dock. An old white sheet lay on the settee bunk with an orange plastic blanket balled up on top of it.

"The Rasta's nest!" I exclaimed.

"Probably," Joyce said. "All he did was smoke pot, write poetry, and play an old guitar. He told me the lights went out, so he was movin' on."

I hit the toggle switch next to the hatch with the picture of a light bulb on it. Nothing. Not a spark in the batteries. The boat had a big diesel, but the starter was scrap metal without electricity, something to think about and deal with later. We also noticed that the doors on the cabins, fore and aft, were not on their hinges. I found all of them in the aft head. It was not part of my experience, at that point, to know that an unsecured companionway door, in rough seas, could swing so violently it will separate itself from the hinges. I believe that was the answer to the mystery.

While I was poking around in the aft cabin, looking for the doors, I discovered a locker full of spare parts and rolls of construction plastic. The parts I understood, but the plastic was a mystery.

"The interior of the boat was lined with that plastic when it came in from South Caicos. My man threw it away because it was full of pot seeds. It keeps them out of the bilge," Joyce said.

"It sure looks like a drug boat," I said.

"It is kind of spooky down below, like a ghost boat," Frankie said.

As we walked about on the deck, I noticed the swage fittings on the shrouds were not the same as the mizzen shrouds. That meant the rigging had been changed at least once. You have to use a boat real hard to wear out stainless rigging to the point of replacement. The once-beautiful cap rails were completely torn off, and I mentioned it to Joyce.

"When they first came in, they tied the boat up to the tire over on the seawall. I think the rails were damaged there."

On my first trip down Long Island Sound, I had tied my old Alden to a pier lined with industrial tires. I arose to find my cap rail had been ground to dust during the night. The combination of a constant swell and some damn tough tires did quick work of the old rotten wooden rails. It appeared that even young teak rails will succumb to a big swell and really tough tires. The belly of the boat had some pretty serious gouges in the gel coat from the tires or the concrete seawall. This damage all indicated a blatant disregard for the cosmetic well-being of the boat. How could any decent upstanding drug smuggler care so little about the appearance of his yacht? I guess you had to walk a mile in their flip-flops.

"Is there a piece of paper and a pencil on the chart table?" Frankie asked.

I jumped down below and returned with the requested items. She laid the paper on a metal plate on the side of the cockpit and, like making a gravestone rubbing, transferred the vital boat information onto the paper, "Jachtwerf Anne Wever B. V., s-Hertogenbosch Holland, hull number 821." None of the words were familiar to me, but I knew a guy in Fort Lauderdale that spoke that language. He had been a yacht broker for enough time in a part of the world where every kind of boat eventually passes through a brokerage.

I shoved the paper in my shorts and suggested we head for town. We scrambled back into the yawl, unrolled the jib, and fell off to starboard. The tide set us astern of the yacht just enough to see the nameboard, *Fortunella III, Antwerp*. Frankie suggested we write the Belgium or Dutch government and maybe Interpol.

"We could try the Coast Guard in Miami also," I said.

Back at the marina hotel, we secured our boat and climbed into the motel's suburban for the tumultuous road trip to the market. The road was cut out of the rocky backbone of the island, about as smooth as the back of an alligator. The suburban knew every hole in the rocky road. Town was a single building that housed the grocery store and the police department. On entering the store, we were amazed at how little food was on the shelves.

"No wonder Chuck brings food directly from Miami," I said to Frankie.

There was not much to choose from, so we picked up some nonfat powdered milk, a pack of hot dogs, and two ice cream sandwiches. Joyce picked us up, with a stack of mail sitting in the back seat, and roared down, perhaps, one of the worst roads I had ever been on. There were mufflers scattered along the highway and a fine assortment of nuts and bolts. The rocks and ruts had created a veritable hardware store in the ditch. No wonder most of the cars on the island were so loud. No muffler shop for six hundred miles.

Frankie and I started back about 2:00 p.m. on a fair tide. I considered sailing along the ocean side of the islands, but the tide was foul in that direction. The tide we were riding was falling, so the bank was getting thinner. Being still new to this particular ocean environment, I was not aware of how thin it would get before the flood tide would lift us again. All was well until the wind began to die. No problem, we still had the motor. Not soon after those thoughts occurred to me, the centerboard started to scrape the coral sand. With no wind, we didn't need the board, so we pulled it up and proceeded to ready the Seagull. Two pulls, and she was off. The motor was off the stern and a bit inconvenient to reach. The process for starting this relic of Dunkirk and D-Day still required a rope with a knot in the end and at least four raps around the exposed flywheel. The rope flew sideways when the spark and piston and gasoline all introduced themselves. The rope hit the top of the float chamber and dislodged it into the ocean. I could see the now-exposed surface of the gas, giggling with the vibration of the running motor. Between the vibration and the minisea sloshing around in the capless container, we were losing a bit of our precious gas into the sea. No spare tops, or anything that looked like a top, so on we went, topless. The motor was making vegetable salad as it ground through the seagrass. The grass and alga were only a small part of the problem—empty conch shells were scattered all over the bottom as well.

"Frankie, keep an eye out for shells and point at any you see."

Just as she stepped forward, the outboard kicked up and revved like the prop had come off. I shut the motor down and jumped overboard. My feet settled into the soft calcium sand. It was knee-deep. The prop spun freely on the driveshaft. This ancient critter was equipped with a big stainless spring wrapped around the shaft. The spring was intended to act as a shear pin. This particular one was now in two separate pieces and without the necessary spring tension to absorb the shock load of a conch encounter that was half-buried in the sand.

It was time to push again. The boat was easy to push with no wind or current. Frankie busied herself looking for anything on the boat that would help to fix the prop. The boat bobbed along happily with its new power source—me. Frankie hung her feet over the side and kicked in a vain attempt to help. It was fun for her, and that did help.

Twenty-three and a half degrees north latitude is the maximum excursion of the sun north of the equator on the first day of summer. It rises due east, arcs directly over your head at noon, and heads due west for the horizon, straight back to the sea. This creates a short day. One minute, it's light, and the next it's dark, no twilight.

We watched the tropical sun settle gently over the island chain to the west of us. We were about four miles short of our destination with the light fading fast. The intention was to press on, but the gathering darkness was far darker than we thought. The islands faded to a shadow and then completely disappeared. No wind, no current, and no horizon; it was time to fish out the anchor, fumble through our groceries for a small dinner, and pull the sail over us for the night. Spam was designed for moments like this. The key comes on the can, it is okay cold, and it fits on a cracker. Never travel away from land without something in a can, especially if it opens without a special device, sold separately.

We lay there in the dark, quiet, listening to the wavelets lap against the clinker hull. Thousands of human beings over the last 1,400 years have lain at anchor on this vast bank of shallow water. The first Indians to arrive in the Caicos Islands were the Lucayans. Their people had migrated north through the West Indies, over many millennia. They were boat people. In Arawak, they called themselves *Lukkune cairi* or "island people." They fished, ate conch, and fashioned pottery for 750 years before an Italian explorer, funded by the new Christian king and queen of Spain, landed on the shores of these or nearby islands.

The Bermudans, French, Spanish, Dominicans, Jamaicans, and the British again have all anchored with Frankie and me on this dark, calm, swimmingly beautiful bank.

Frankie was the first to notice the luminescent green glow in the water around the boat. We hung on the gunnels and gazed at a biological display of palolo worms performing their monthly love drama. The female worms start the evening, about fifty minutes after sunset, with a spiral dance near the surface. The males, safely parked on the bottom, launch a water-jet-powered sperm package upward at the spiraling females. The sperm missile collides with the swimming female and causes her to release a cloud of eggs, which are mixed with the incoming sperm. This light show is enhanced by the fact that all the worms and their sexual equipment are bioluminescent. There is a mention of this effect in Columbus' journal. It was just "lights in the water" to Chris. It took scientists a while to figure out the rest. All we could do or know at the time was, it was nature at her best. The water lights ended as quickly as they began, and we went to sleep.

Sunrise put enough water on the bank to float us off the bottom. Both of us unwrapped ourselves from the sail, rerigged it to the mast, and caught the early breeze on a nice reach along the back side of the cay to the cut and home.

Chuck was standing on the dock to handle our lines as we made our last tack and slid into the slip.

Ronald White

"You can't be a real islander until you spend a night out on the bank."

"I guess we are members of the club now," I said.

Frankie was a little less philosophical; she needed a shower and some dry clothes. It was a nice adventure, especially since the weather was in a good mood. I told Chuck about the luminescent critters around the boat after the sun set. He was aware of the phenomena and clued us in on the fireworms. I scratched around through some invertebrate zoology text to find the fireworm or *Odontosyllis luminosa* and its sexual habits. In the '70s, biological field guides were illustrated with hand sketches or black-and-white pictures. Birds were well covered by *Golden* books and *Peterson Field Guides*. The well-equipped biology student owned as many field guides as their lifestyle would accommodate. A smartphone is a lot lighter.

Sunshine Is Not Enough

The tropical winter at 22.5 degrees north latitude is warm, day and night, with an occasional dying cold front for punctuation. It takes a little creativity to wake up each day with a plan, especially if there is a little self-motivation parked in your genes. Each and every one of the PRIDE crew harbored this gene. No one slept in, so the days were long, and our conversations on conservation and development were seldom casual.

As a linguist, Frankie was not as emotionally involved in the foundation as the rest of us. She spent time with the native employees, coaching them on English grammar and writing. She drew a small salary for this work and enjoyed the time she spent with Raymond and Dolphus. After breakfast, she would spend time with either Stevie or Kathy or both. Strong female personalities grazed and played together day after day, with limited activities beyond our close environment. An island, by definition, is a chunk of land surrounded by water. Did I mention our chunk was only eight hundred acres? Our female companions were all talented modern women living in a fishbowl with clear walls and limited possibilities. The beach and the tennis court were not enough beyond the structured daily chores.

Gossip was an endemic form of conversation, leaving little undiscovered when it came to sleeping arrangements and pillow talk. I had no idea that my discretion with the college student, prior to Frankie's arrival, would become an indiscretion and fodder for the island gristmill. There were, of course, indiscretions perpetrated by the gossipers that were never mentioned. The target species (gender) was generally the bucks. We (the bucks) fiddled with all the gadgetry that allowed us to live our day-to-day lives, in relative comfort, six hundred miles offshore from the big island (the USA).

Meanwhile, idle conversation disclosed a perceived previous indiscretion by me, and Frankie was informed. This information weakened our relationship enough that she decided to head back to the States. This decision was not what I had planned. Going it alone was hard to reconcile since the politics of the island were also wearing me down. Her departure gave me the shove I needed to move in the direction I had intended to when I first traveled to the West Indies.

A family from Vermont aided my departure. With the loan of an inflatable boat equipped with an outboard motor, I loaded my gear and guitar into the boat and set off for Provo. I was greeted by Calvin the cook and welcomed to his island.

DON BOSCO OR LA BASCADORO

Before Frankie's final departure, we had traveled to Miami for a short break from paradise. We had composed a letter to the US Coast Guard and the Belgian government. The letter described the boat we had found and all the pertinent information we had gleaned from the locals. The broker in Fort Lauderdale let me know the brand of the boat, made by Anne Wever. *Trintella IV* was her model, and her name was *Fortunella III*. The Belgians wrote back with some confusion, having mixed up the brand with the name. They found no Fortunella named *Trintella III*. Ah well, we tried in French but not Flemish.

The Coast Guard, fluent in the same language as Frankie and I, found the theft records for the vessel and graced us with the owner's name, address, and phone number in Antwerp. On a second trip to the boat, we had also found a single phone number on a sheet of carbon paper in the chart table. This number haunted me a little, but I did manage to screw my courage up and make the call. The voice on the line was immediately concerned about my identity. Straightaway, I confessed my interest in the boat and inquired about the presence of the phone number on the boat. The voice told me he was an employee of the owner and just part of the delivery crew.

I pushed him to tell me how to get in touch with the owner, and he verbally backed up and told me the owner was very difficult to contact, and he would let him know about my interest as soon as he called. I was talking to a very paranoid and, perhaps, drug-altered male, located in South Florida. In the old days, an area code covered several counties. After I hung up the phone, I called the operator to find out which town the call was made to. The operator feigned concern that I wanted that information and then gave it up. Having overheard another voice in the background, calling "hey, Roger" to the man on the phone, we now knew that the guy's name was Roger, and he lived in Okeechobee, Florida. The first time we went aboard the boat, I found two round-trip airline tickets from Miami to Cape Haitian and back. The return trip was unused for Jim Thomson and Roger Pigeon. I think we had found our Roger.

Three phone calls, easily made from a pay phone in Miami, had netted us a wealth of information. The fourth call was to Belgium and, with great hope, to the owner. When I spoke in English, the voice answered in English. What a relief. I immediately let the person know that I knew the location of his boat. The person identified himself as Mr. Bremer's manager. I took that at face value. He explained to me that Mr. B was in Greece visiting a wine festival but would be traveling back to a boat in Martinique when he was finished tasting wine. This was the second person in an hour to tell me that the owner was very difficult to contact. There was no way to tell if the "manager" or Roger knew each other. Mr. B's manager mentioned that the boat's name was *Don Bosco*, and it was somewhere near Pointe Du Bout, on the island of Martinique. The condo we were staying in was adjacent to the Dadeland Mall in South Miami. We walked across a footbridge to the rear of the mall where we found a bookstore near the food plaza. The travel section provided us with a tourist guide to the French West Indies. Pointe Du Bout had only one boatel, so we jotted the number down and headed on back to the condo.

My parents lived across the State on the West Coast. They had not met Frankie, so I decided to visit them and stop in Okeechobee on the way. We were both excited and intrigued to see if we could find out where Roger Pigeon lived and maybe sneak a peek. Okeechobee is located on the north shore of the lake of the same name. There was no doubt that the big shallow lake was a perfect drop zone and retrieval basin for all kinds of illicit farm products from South America. Our first stop was the voter registration office. The clerk was helpful but found no voter named Roger Pigeon. What were we thinking? Drug smugglers do not vote, but they do use water and sewer.

The town hall had Mr. Pigeon in three residences in just four years. The first was a trailer, then an apartment, and finally a brick ranch in an upscale neighborhood. We had an address. In ten minutes, we were driving slowly by the brick ranch, craning through the car window for a good look. No curtains or car. I stopped a block away and walked up to the house. Without curtains, I could see the rooms had no furniture. The house had been evacuated within twenty-four hours of my last call. We found a phone booth and placed the same call to Roger's number and got a recording.

"We are sorry, this number is no longer in service," the operator said. Wow, somebody was paranoid. With one phone call from a strange person—me—Roger and his cohorts had packed up and scurried into the dark.

"What a way to live," I said to Frankie. Little did I know I would adopt the same tactic in my own near future?

It was time to head back to Miami and make the call to Martinique. We were both quiet as we drove back, thinking about the abandoned house and the possibility of contacting the owner of the boat. The doubt about his relationship with the strange people on the phone was very real. We just could not put the two together.

As we drove along the two-lane road, around the north rim of the lake, a Jimmy Buffet song came to mind. "When I ruled my world from a phone booth" were the words from the *Coconut Telegraph* album, and I was sure doing that right now. We parked the old Toyota truck in the condo parking lot, in the same spot it had been sitting for the last six months. Somehow, while I had been on the island, they had managed to resurface the entire lot, including the spot we were parked in. I never figured out how they could, or would, move an old truck somehow and paint the asphalt and then put it back. We were in Miami, where stealing the truck would be the most efficient means of painting the parking lot.

We walked to the phone booth at the pool and placed a stack of quarters on the metal shelf. The operator instructed me to put $7 in the phone to place a call to the French West Indies. Back then, pay as you go was how you went. I punched in the number, and the phone started ringing.

"*Bon jour, comment tale vu.*"

"Hello, do you speak English?"

"Yes."

"Do you have a guest named Hugo Bremer?"

"*Mais oui*, he is right here."

I looked at Frankie and whispered, "He is at the desk."

The desk clerk handed the phone to Hugo.

"Hello, who is this?"

I could not believe, after months of intrigue and misguidance, I was about to talk to the owner of the boat.

"Hello, Mr. Bremer, my name is Ron White, and I have found your boat."

"Which boat would that be?"

"*Fortunella III*, from Antwerp, Belgium. It is in the Turks and Caicos Islands."

"I'm not sure I know where that is."

I went on to explain, as best I could, the boat's location and why I knew it was there. It was also pertinent to let him know how far away the boat was from him and what form of transportation he might use to get to me and the boat. It was my impression that he intended to sail the vessel he was on to the Turks and Caicos Islands in the near future. It could not take more than a week to sail down-wind from Martinique to Provo, even if you are sightseeing. This was another reason I planned to leave Pine Cay. Connecting with Hugo was my primary imperative.

Hugo assured me that he would head my way and be there by the twentieth of April. He told me the name of his boat was *Don Bosco*. It seemed like a strange name for a boat, but what did I know, especially about European boat names. *Fortunella* was not exactly the most common name in the marina. I later learned that *Fortunella* was the name of an Italian movie released in 1958 and directed by Fellini. It is also a species of a Chinese kumquat brought to England by a guy named Robert Fortune.

Why Did the Cook Leave So Soon?

I moved aboard *Fortunella* and set to work repairing the Zodiac folded on the back deck. Duct tape and BoatLIFE will repair almost anything, so I started the glue-and-tape game that lasted until the day I sold the Zodiac to another poor soul. The next job was to get the batteries out of the engine room and take them ashore and hooked up to a power source for rebirth. The process required using the main boom and tackle to raise three two-hundred-pound batteries, one at a time, from the engine room over the side and into the semirepaired inflatable. Three batteries, a six-horsepower outboard motor, and myself were quite a load for the inflatable. With Calvin's help, I managed to get the batteries out of the boat just before the rubber boat sunk. This became an ongoing struggle with the boat's ability to hold air and my ability to give it enough air to maintain rigidity.

Three big batteries back in the box, the hot wire, and the negative wire firmly attached energized the electrical system, and on came the lights. There were lights everywhere. *Fortunella* was alive and well.

The next thing I wanted to do was get the engine started and go for a ride. The ignition key was mounted outside on the steering station, looking at the stars. The ketch had crossed the Atlantic, thrashing around in heavy seas and rain. A dollop of seawater splashed into the key slot will pretty much destroy any key mechanism, even a marine one. This one was frozen solid. I disconnected the wires and proceeded to hot-wire the boat, and—*vroom*—the engine kicked right off. Startled, I ran to the bow and hauled the anchor up as the bow fell off, and away we went. Pushing the throttle forward kicked the boat into high gear, *Fortunella* steamed around the anchorage at a high rate of speed. *Whoa, a sailboat that motors like a powerboat*, I thought. The engine started to pick up rpm, which seemed strange to me, and then it just died. Another trip to the bow to reanchor, and down into the engine room for a look. Oh shit, the fuel valves—both of them—were shut off. Not knowing much about diesels, I tried to start the engine again. No success.

It was time to refer to the book. Amazingly the English owner's manual was written in delightful prose with lots of commentary on the possible situations one might be in, if one was reading this part of the manual.

> In the event that you run the engine out of fuel, you must purge the system of air with new fuel sourced from the mechanical pump attached to the bottom of the lift pump. It is advised that you wear a glove or place a Band-Aid on your pump finger. You will most assuredly wear a hole in the glove or the Band-Aid during the pumping process. But not your finger.

I did neither and wore a hole in my finger. It took the rest of the day to complete the meticulous instructions in the manual. It informed me that failure to do so would deplete the batteries and require the hoisting of the distress signal, "which all well-equipped yachts would certainly have on board."

The engine did start without depleting the batteries, and I can assure you, I never went tooting around any harbor again without checking the position of the fuel valves. This was my first lesson in diesel mechanics and certainly not my last. I also confirmed the presence of the distress flag on board. Nowadays one would witness the dawn of a new Ice Age while waiting for a response from a properly hoisted distress signal flag. When I finally got to the States in the boat, I replaced the manual lift pump with an automotive electric fuel pump. Bleeding the fuel system after that was a breeze.

I settled into a new life in Leeward Going Through and became acquainted with a list of seminefarious characters in the marina. No one was who they said they were or did what they said they did. Calvin and I seemed to be the only actors actually playing ourselves. There were two guys on a twenty-something-foot go-fast boat, partying and diving for lobsters. Their flimsy little production boat could bop along at sixty miles per hour if the ocean was flat. That's a ten-hour trip from Miami if the seats stay bolted to the floor. It seemed a long way to travel for a few lobsters. The twin 235-horsepower engines were the biggest outboards ever made. The Miami boat show had made a big splash with these new motors, and everyone with an extra helping of testosterone was sporting a couple of these bad boys on their transom. There was another boat, named *Solid Gold*, in the marina bragging that they were a test boat for Evinrude. They were traveling from Saint Thomas to Newport, Rhode Island, by outboard motorboat. The manufacturer thought it would be a great publicity stunt. The two *Solid Gold* guys and the two guys from Florida spent a lot of time playing pool and smoking dope. No one was in a hurry to get back to Florida or Rhode Island.

The cast of characters around the marina and hotel was changing all the time. A group of New York-type guys checked into the hotel for a fishing-and-drinking vacation. The hotel offered a twenty-five-foot fiberglass boat with a local captain for a guide. At the end of a day of fishing, the usual plan was for the captain/mate to clean a few of the fish for the charters and receive payment and the rest of the fish to carry home with him. The biggest guy in the charter party, dressed in a black Speedo, black cowboy boots, and matching black hat, started to give the captain a hard time about the division of the fish. Joyce, the manager of the marina and hotel, was in town, so I asked Calvin if the captain's position was unreasonable.

"Fresh fish is the best tip in the islands, mon," Calvin said. "You just end up buying the fish with the money anyway."

I asked Calvin if he thought he could lift the cowboy over his head.

"Sure, mon, I'll give it a try."

I quickly grabbed my camera as Calvin moved like a jungle cat toward the "wise guy." Up he went, straight over the cook's head. I clicked a picture, and everyone broke into a smile. A tense situation had turned into a humorous guy thing. The other wise guys thought it was hilarious to see their buddy floating above Calvin's massive head. Calvin put him down and told him he would cook their fish for dinner.

The next day, Joyce had heard about the incident and asked me if I would stay long enough to stand in for her while she went back to England on holiday. I agreed to be the acting marina manager for a while. Hugo would not be here for a couple of weeks. I had the time, and I could use the money. She planned to leave her teenage daughter at the hotel in my care. The daughter was a bit of a souse, but that was not any of my business, or so I thought.

My routine was to anchor the boat near the inlet in the evening to maximize the breeze and sweep the boat of mosquitoes. After several horrible nights near the mangroves and the bugs, anchoring in the breeze was a great relief. I would haul anchor in the morning and motor over near the marina just so the trip in the inflatable was short enough to make the dock on one trick at the foot pump.

Just as I started my morning drill, the radio crackled into life.

"Leeward Marina, Leeward Marina, this is *La Bascadoro*, come back."

Since I was the marina guy now, I realized I was the one to answer the radio. The problem was, I immediately realized that this could be Hugo. Were the mob guys staying at the marina part of Hugo's operation? Was *La Bascadoro* and *Don Bosco* the same boat? Could this all be a really big coincidence?

I picked up the mic and responded, "This is Leeward Marina. How can I help you?"

They needed help getting through the reef and over the outer bar. I gave them the info they needed while noting that the captain was speaking with an American accent. I quickly anchored *Fortunella* and jumped into the partially inflated rubber boat. There was no time to pump her up, so I motored to the dock with the transom tilting back at a forty-five-degree angle. Kelly, Joyce's daughter, helped me with the bowline as I scrambled to the top of the concrete pier.

"Kelly, do me a favor. When this boat comes in, greet them and see if there is a guy named Hugo on board."

This probably seemed strange to her, but my paranoia meter was reading 90 percent, and I was on the verge of fight or flight. I hustled off to the office to handle the radio while Kelly and Calvin handled their dock lines. The vessel came into the harbor with all the grace of a yacht belonging to British royalty. She was a fifty-or-so-year-old wooden hull with gleaming varnish and a round reversed transom that cascaded to the waterline with shimmering brightwork. Someone had poured money into a magnificent restoration of a grand old vessel. Was this Hugo? The crew seemed well-muscled to the extreme. The bow came off the current, and the captain pulled the stern to the dock. The largest of the crew hefted a huge anchor and heaved it up current to kedge the bow off the dock. As soon as the lines were fast, barbells were brought over the varnished rail and onto the pier. I could see Kelly in animated conversation with the captain. *Good girl*, I thought.

She came over to the radio shack and unceremoniously announced, "No Hugo."

I was relieved but not convinced. I was looking down the dock at muscle beach party on a yacht. When do you see the crew of a yacht hop off, as soon the boat is tied up, and set up a portable gym? Someone had to greet the captain, so off I went. The captain was well cultured and well-heeled. He showed me the scuba room with compressor and fall system, a great main cabin with a built-in stereo system and lots of leather upholstery. It was quite splendid. The only woman on board was the cook. She was right off the cover of one of those bodybuilding magazines you see in the supermarket. She was better than the magazine.

The owner asked me, "Is there any entertainment on the island?"

"Yeah, it's in town, at the Third Turtle Inn. It's just me and another guy. I play the guitar and sing, the other guy just laughs and criticizes me, I'm the straight guy."

"Can we get a ride in when you go?"

"Sure, I will honk the horn when we are about to leave."

I asked Kelly for the keys to the suburban, and she hopped into the driver's seat. *Oh, what the heck*, I thought, *she hasn't had that much to drink this afternoon.*

I told her to honk the horn. The hard bodies piled into the back two rows of seats, and away we went. Seventy miles an hour, along the back of a dinosaur, is way too fast. Kelly had been on the bottle, so I should have been the driver. It was a miracle that the wheels were still on the car when we arrived at the Third Turtle. I told the crowd to follow Kelly to the bar; I was going to the eat-and-entertainment part of the inn, which they were more than welcome to drift over to, after they got enough booze.

Sandy, the comedian, and I had done this act a couple of times, so we just kicked back and let it happen. He always explained that he was an itinerant golf pro and gardener with sex privileges for a Russian duchess over on Parrot Cay. That always got a laugh. We had been told that an author named Benchley and a model named Cheryl Tiegs were there that night, so we were doing our best to do our best. That wasn't very good, but it was all we (everyone on the island) had.

We were on our third song when a loud crash erupted from the bar. The barbell boys, Kelly, and the cook were the only ones in there, or at least that's what I thought. I threw my guitar in the case and ran into the bar. The room was being turned into a lumberyard by the table-wielding muscle dudes. A few drunken sailors were lying bloodied on the floor, and Kelly was motioning me to the side door.

I yelled, "The marina car is heading back right now."

Everyone we came with flooded into the car, with Kelly at the wheel again. She was really stoked by now, so the ride back was even more terrifying. As we careened along the rock-studded road, the reason for the disturbance in the bar became clear. An unfortunate sailor had made a pass at the cook, which her boyfriend did not like. As this thought was jelling in my head, the cook was peeling the shirt and a lot of the boyfriend's skin off in the back of the car. The wild motion of the vehicle and the even-wilder motion of the cook's hands created a maniacal scene. We screeched to a halt at the marina, and the entire crowd dashed out of the car and headed for their boat. I pointed Kelly toward her door and retired to my boat for the night.

The next morning, I was met at the dock by the skipper of the yacht. He wanted to know if I could get a taxi so the cook could get to the airport ASAP. Too much testosterone and not enough estrogen, I wonder who cooked for them on their way to the Amazon. They told me they were going to do charters there, imagine that!

Bon Voyage

Joyce returned just in time to run block between the local sheriff and me. He was very interested in my intentions for *Fortunella*. I do not know what she said, but it kept him at bay for a while. It was not the first time he had come to question me, and I was sure it would not be the last. I bummed a ride to town, and the first person I ran into was the customs official. He told me he had no concern about the boat, but I should consider dealing with the boat somewhere else. He suggested I come by, and he would give me my clearance papers the next day. While I was at the store, I ran into a Canadian fellow named Danney, who had arrived on a southbound boat. He was low on cash and needed a ride to Miami, I might need a crew.

I ran into Mark the Nark when I got back to the marina. He asked me if I planned to leave soon. I, of course, asked why. He explained that it might be safer to deal with the boat in Miami. Mark was in the know, so to speak, being a not-so-undercover agent. Miami was becoming a no-brainer. I went out to *Fortunella* and hailed the boat Danny was on, on the VHF radio. I let him know I was planning to leave the next day late in the afternoon. Danny was concerned about the difficulty of the channel in poor light conditions. I told him I had a plan.

At first light, I pumped the inflatable as tight as I could and headed for the marina. There was a good supply of bricks around the docks and a pile of milk jugs behind the kitchen. A little string from Calvin, and I was prepared to mark the channel all the way to the reef. I told Calvin we were headed for the Virgin Islands to find Hugo. It's always good to throw off your pursuers by 180 degrees, at least. I gave him my dad's phone number in the States and thanked him for all his support and help. Calvin was the best human being I knew at the time.

Danny arrived late in the afternoon the next day. The word around the marina was, something was going to happen the next day. The sheriff had been by again, but I managed to stay out on the boat until he left. It was time to go.

Danny and I hoisted the anchor at 4:00 a.m. and began following the milk jugs back and forth through the coral heads until we reached the breach in the reef and the open sea. The first swell lifted the bow skyward, and we crashed into the tropical Atlantic with twelve thousand feet of water under us. *Fortunella* shouldered into the oncoming waves with the joy of years of human boat designers. How can we make it faster, safer, and more comfortable, is the mantra of the marine architect. Mr. E. G. Van-De-Stadt had done a splendid job of designing this boat.

The boat had the heft and power to exhilarate the hell out of me. I was in love.

We made the sixty miles to Mayaguana by early afternoon and dropped anchor on the south side of the island in a little bay. We had enough lee to get out of the southeast swell.

Laying to a swell with the sails down is not pleasant unless you like your coffee in your lap every time a wave hits the beam of the boat. We went snorkeling and speared a triggerfish for dinner. Combined with some conch meat and a can of beans, we were in fine shape.

We hauled anchor the next morning and headed north toward George Town in the southern Exumas. We would pass by the Plana Cays, Auckland's Island, and Long Island during the next two days. The Plana Cays have no human population, but they do have a medium-size rabbitlike rodent known to the locals as hutia. They are ravenous vegetarians, which controls their population. They have been there for millions of years, so I guess the balance between weeds and weed-eaters is working. A well-meaning Englishman scattered the little plant-munching critters on islands with iguanas on them further north in the Exuma Cays. This may be a limiting factor for the rodents and the lizards since they both prefer the vegan way.

On the second night out, the sunset revealed a curtain of lightning to the north on our course. Hauling down a mainsail in sixty knots of wind during a squall was not my idea of a good time. The boat had to be brought into the wind for this maneuver. The vessel generally is not happy when this has to happen, and neither is the crew. I told Danny that the mainsail should be struck for the duration of the night, and we would sail with the mizzen and the jib. Danny was not happy with this plan and expressed his disapproval. I informed him that I was the captain, and the sail was coming down. We furled the sail and paid off before the wind again. The log read six knots. Not bad without the main. I settled into the makeshift seat we had fashioned from a cushion, and the door from the forward head propped up as a seat back.

Everything was well until I remembered the radio transmission I had heard earlier in the day. A voice came across the air.

"Key West Coast Guard, we are northwest of your position, and the wind is blowing over ninety knots, over."

The voice faded after that, but it sure was strange to get a transmission from an island over three hundred miles away about a storm that might be heading our way. All the more reason to have the mainsail secured. I was listening to a song on the radio called "Against the Wind" out of a station in Virginia Beach. That was at least two thousand miles from my position. AM radio stations blast their signal out at fifty thousand watts. The signal then bounces between the ionosphere and the earth ricocheting out thousands of miles. Mariners far out to sea can listen to stations all over the world if they have an AM radio. The signal from the Key West boat was transmitted on FM. The only reason I heard the signal, three hundred miles away, probably had to do with the weather system between me and the vessel off Key West.

The wind went slack for a moment and then veered to the north and increased rapidly to about eighty knots. I jumped up to release the jib sheet just as the sail blew into pieces. I felt something hit me on the head and realized the stainless rib holding the vinyl dodger top was lying behind me, and the vinyl top was completely gone. I then noticed a light right next to the boat on what looked like a huge balloon. It took me a few seconds to realize that it was the life raft, fully inflated and struggling to get loose from its inflation rope. Seconds later, it tumbled off into the spume of rain and sea-foam.

"Danny, Danny, get up here and help me. I have to get what is left of the jib down."

No answer. I jumped down below and was shocked to step into calf-deep water on the cabin floor. I hit the light and saw Danny pushing on the leeward porthole.

"Damn, the ports are open!"

I pushed past Danny to the second port and grabbed it with both hands and pulled down as hard as I could. Managing to slip the dog over the yoke on the port, I screwed it down and did the same to the other side. We both collapsed on the bunk now that the ocean was not pouring into the aft cabin at such an alarming rate. The water was receding on the floor, so the pump must have been working.

We were still heeled over, but it seemed nice inside without the rain and wind. I flipped the spreader lights on to look at the damage. The jib had flogged itself to pieces.

The mizzen must still be up, or we would be thrashing around a lot more, I thought. The speedometer was visible from the hatch. It was sitting on nine knots, and we seemed to be tracking in a constant direction. Hauling myself out of the cabin into the cockpit, I could see the mizzen was up and pulling. We were on a broad reach, in huge seas, making great time, our heading was northwest. That's as good as it gets. I let the mizzen out just a bit to reduce our heel and yelled to Danny. "Want some coffee and a couple of eggs?"

He piled into the galley, and we proceeded to cook breakfast at nine knots on a constant heading that the boat had decided on. We were clear of land and in eight thousand feet of water. The boat had settled into a point of sail that made us all happy. Within an hour, the wind subsided to about twenty knots and then down to almost nothing by the time the sun came up. We had closed on land to the northwest, which gave us a lee and very little wave action. It was smooth sailing.

It was time to let Danny know that opening the ports in the open ocean was not a good idea. I didn't bother. He certainly knew it by now. I later removed the opening ports from the aft cabin and replaced them with deadlights, or nonopening portholes.

We sailed around Cape Santa Maria on the north end of Long Island and in the general direction of George Town, in the southern Exhumes. Mark the Narc had loaned me his copy of *The Bahamas*

Cruising Guide. Yes, Mark was looking out for me. I mused on the difficulty of threading through the patch reefs and outcroppings in good or bad weather. Harry Kline, the author of the *Bahamas Guide*, had, with the help of a whole lot of people, charted every sunker and head worth hitting with a six-foot draft vessel. *Fortunella* was less drafty at 5'3"; I took no chances and followed Harry's directions to the tee. We weaved in and out of the channel until we finally arrived off the town dock and anchored.

My first view of the Elizabeth Harbour revealed what looked like a forest of sailboat masts all bunched together on the back side of Stocking Island. With the help of binoculars, I realized that the winter fleet of cruising boats from the US and Canada were pushed up on the beach in a horrific pile. The hurricane-force winds from yesterday's storm certainly caught everyone sleeping and unaware. Some vessels were cast onto the rocky exterior of the island, and the rest lay against them or were stranded in shallow water by the depth of their keels. Several hundred vessels were in need of commercial assistance.

Danny, on the other hand, was responding to the reggae music dancing across the azure-blue water from the town. As the sun set, I thought it best to wait until business hours the next day to clear customs. The overtime charges can be hefty, especially if the agent is just sitting down to dinner. Danny was enthralled by the music and the possibility of dancing with the young native girls. I informed him that we were in a new country, and the protocol was to ask permission to enter before we went ashore. We made dinner out of the canned food locker, and I settled down with a book to await the dawn. Danny departed with a splash from the back deck and went dancing. I had informed him it was highly illegal to enter without permission, and I would disavow any knowledge of who he was, or where he came from, but he swam ashore anyway.

I motored *Fortunella* to the dock the next morning. I went ashore to find the customs man or the phone to call his office. After I made contact, I returned to the long-heaving dock and merged with Danny, returning from a night of debauchery ashore. He was relieved to see me smile a bit as I hurried him down the dock and back on to the boat. The smile was my recognition of how hungover he looked.

He certainly was not the first or last to jump ship for a party, and I was relieved that no one noticed.

The tropical sun was just getting up ahead of steam when I noticed a large Bahamian gentleman standing on the deck with a broad smile. "Where were you fellas when it blew so hard?"

"We were off shore where it was safe," I said.

He reared back in a huge laugh.

"This must be some strong boat."

I agreed and welcomed him on board. He came down into the main cabin like he was in his own living room.

"You fellas comin' from the south?"

"Yes, mon, the Turks and Caicos. We are passing through to Miami."

Knowing that the locker was well stocked with a variety of alcohol, I reached in and presented him with a fine bottle of Rhum Barbancourt from Haiti. This was better than gold. He asked me to fill out the routine paperwork and present ownership of the vessel. Now this was a problem I had anticipated back in Provo. I asked Frankie to send me a fax to the small international headquarters of several hundred US corporations housed in a twelve-foot-by-twelve-foot-cement bunker at the marina. A local girl was the sole secretary for this entire operation and receiver of fax mail. She had sent me a fax ostensibly from the owner giving me permission to deliver the vessel *Fortunella* to Miami and signed it *Hugo Bremer*. The agent looked at the letter.

"You are not the same fellas that usually run this boat, are you?"

"No, the owner is done with that kind of stuff now," I replied.

He got up and walked forward into the forecastle, returned, and smiled again. "You fellas have a nice trip, my wife and I will sure enjoy this rum."

I held steady when he went forward to search the boat. If I had flinched, his departure would have been delayed for sure. We were not carrying anything illegal, and all crew was present and accounted for. What a relief!

DINING WITH KINGS

Now that we were legally in the Bahamas, we made a trip up the street to the grocery store from the customs dock. Just as I suspected, the store had very little variety but lots of character and as many characters. While I was staring at a $6 jar of peanut butter, a Hispanic gentleman excused himself and took a jar off the shelf. I couldn't help notice the valise handcuffed to his wrist. The store prices were high but not that high. I guess he had trust issues with the crew he was traveling with, by air or sea. Like Provo, George Town had a harbor and an airport, another drug junction.

Communications in the third world were almost nonexistent at the time, but it still seemed like a quick departure might be in order. A small corner of my imagination harbored thoughts of collusion among the smugglers. Once at sea, we were safe again.

With our guidebook in hand, we left Elizabeth Harbour and headed north up the Exuma chain. Sailing along the chain of low, mostly uninhabited, islands was a lot of guesswork. There are no inlet markers of any kind, each hill looks the same, and houses or man-made landmarks come and go with the wind.

My plan was to sail until we were very sure of the inlet name and depth because I was not sure of my position most of the time.

We started trailing a big feathered hook on a Cuban doughnut behind the boat in the hopes of fish for dinner. The fishing reel was a plastic ring wrapped with a hundred feet of heavy cord. The fisherman throws the weighted line into the water, and the line loops off the doughnut. You just wrap the line back on the spool to reel it in. No gears, no handles, no lube, no hassles. The third world everywhere uses the rig and catches just as many fish as the guy with the

Abercrombie and Fitch deep-sea rod and all the stuff that streams out the store with it.

Danny was on the back deck berating me and my primitive fishing gear when *wham*, a very large dolphin took the hook. Danny took the tack of just dragging the fish in by hand without the effort of coiling it onto the reel. He hooted and shouted as the deep-sea fish charged into the air and crashed to the surface again and again. The fishing line began to pile on the deck until I arrived with the gaff hook and brought the fish onto the boat. The fish hit the deck gushing blood and pounding the wood deck like a sledgehammer. I dove on the head, and Danny sat on the tail. Blue, gold, and red rippled through the sides of the fish as the life left him. The Spanish refer to this fish as the El Dorado or city of gold. It is well named and deserves all the accolades of a star athlete. We were covered with blood and fish slime and totally exhausted. This was more fish than we could eat, so I cut half the fillet into strips for salting and drying. The rest would be dinner.

All this fishing had brought both of us to the back deck, away from the wheel. As I was looking around to get my bearings, I noticed a red flare make a short arc and land in the sea. I brought *Fortunella* around on a course to intercept the position of the flare. A small vessel was just below the horizon. As we approached, I could see several people waving their arms. Finally, I could see the lettering on the side of the boat—*Solid Gold*. Yup, the same boat that was in the marina back in Provo.

The two guys with the hairy chests and uncountable gold bracelets and necklaces were all grins when we came alongside.

"We ran out of gas," the helmsmen said. "How about a tow?"

Danny took a bowline, and we returned to our northerly course. Our two hairy friends turned up the stereo and relaxed as we, the turtle, towed the hare to the finish line.

Back on course, I spotted a break in the coastal cliff that should lead us into a magic harbor on the back side of Staniel Cay. The guidebook dedicated four pages to this stop, and we were excited. There is a cave with an underwater grotto right in the middle of the bay. A great old English yacht club bar, dripping with history, and two stores—a blue one and a pink one—were the spots to shop and drink. The book also mentioned an ice machine. That's the stuff in your rum and coke that makes that tingling sound when you swirl your glass. I had not heard that sound for a while. We swung into the fuel dock with the go-fast boat in tow and secured our dock lines. The fuel guy came over and helped our new friends get fueled up and ready to head toward Newport, Rhode Island. I told the captain we were going to anchor off for the night. He thanked me profusely and slipped a roll of bills into my hand.

I stuffed the roll in my pocket and said, "Oh, you don't have to do that."

He insisted. They both headed for the bar, and we cast off and anchored with the antique lump of cast iron that came with the boat. It had let me down many times, but it was all I had, so down it went. I knew we could not eat all the fish we had on board so I got on the radio and let everybody in the harbor know that we had fish to share or trade. Danny insisted we pump up the inflatable and go ashore for a drink. He started pumping while I answered the radio call to *Fortunella* from one of the other boats in the harbor. The boat calling was at the main dock and was interest in the fish. In fact, they invited us to go and dine with them. This meant shirt and shoes, but we were up for it. I dropped down below to locate my shoes and search for a clean pair of shorts. I dumped the contents of my pocket on the bunk and noticed the top bill in the roll was a hundred dollars. I unrolled the rest of the bills to find they were all hundreds, all ten of them. I have no idea what they were up to, but they were sure glad to see us.

The shore boat was losing air almost as fast as Danny could pump. I paddled like a madman against the current for ten minutes before we reached the dock. As we pulled up to the pier, a guy in a white chef outfit helped us tie up. He introduced himself and indicated the boat we were to dine on was the one taking up the entire pier. That was at least a one-hundred-foot boat. He escorted us, and our fish, to the gangway and took our fish onto the boat while inviting us into the main salon. Two well-dressed very-good-looking women offered us drinks, sat us down, and asked if we were interested in seeing a video. Neither of us had heard of a video movie on television. In fact, I had not even seen a TV for months. We sat and watched a film called *American Graffiti* on TV until the dinner was ready. We sat down with fresh drinks, still admiring the lovely women, and greeted the owner as he sat at the head of the large table. He introduced himself as George and thanked us for the fish. The conversation was mostly about our trip so far and almost nothing about him. When he finished his meal, he excused himself and politely left. We finished the meal and rose to leave. One of the women again thanked us for the fish. As we approached the cabin door, I asked what George's last name was.

"Oh, his name is Constantine."

I knew immediately that we had just eaten with the king of Greece. What I didn't know was that he had been forced out of power back in Greece and was now living in the Bahamas in exile. The dinner was great, and we had been introduced to VCR technology.

I perused the guidebook the next morning to get an idea about Staniel Cay and the surrounding area. There was a very large mass of rock, about twenty feet high and two hundred feet in diameter, in the middle of the bay. There seemed to be some snorkeling activity on the west side. The book said the island was hollow with a hole right at the top. The sun would shine through the hole into the grotto of crystal-clear water at noon and illuminate the underwater cave. It was the cave that Ursula Andreas and Sean Connery emerged from at the end of the *Thunderball* movie. We had to go see that.

We fumbled with the rubber boat and the undependable outboard and finally rowed over to the cave with less-than-adequate buoyancy in the boat. I threw the painter into the water and dove down to secure it to a piece of coral on the bottom. While I was there, I noticed a long moving orange-and-white tail, or taillike, living thing at the bottom in front of me. Of course, I touched it, and it slithered across the bottom and withdrew under a rock. The animal was at least ten feet long and somehow parked under that rock. The next vision was the incredible number of huge reef fish swimming at the entrance of the cave. I had never seen marine life so large or so tame. This little grotto was a marine sanctuary established by the Bahamian government. I was used to viewing tropical reefs heavily fished by spears and traps. It's humbling to experience a pristine environment allowed to prosper by itself. This was Danny's first ride in paradise. He could only think it was like this everywhere; if only it was.

We surfaced inside the cave and climbed onto a thin ledge just above the surface of the water. The sun cast a golden beam of light down into the water from the hole above our heads. We lay on the ledge surrounded by rock and water, like two lungfish fresh from the sea. We slithered into the water and emerged on the east side of the grotto, like Sean and Ursula, into the sunlight.

Back on the boat, I checked my invertebrate key and discovered that the taillike critter I had spotted was a tiger tail sea cucumber. In all the thousands of hours I have spent underwater since that day, I have never seen another specimen like that one. Carpe diem.

I chose the ocean side of the islands for our northern passage because the water was eight thousand feet deep with lots of hungry fish. The inside passage is festooned with rocky sand ridges and coral heads. It's easier to be off your toes and fishing than to be on your toes, waiting for the thump of hard bottom under the keel.

We spent the next night in Highbourne Cay and then on to Nassau. The eastern entrance to Nassau, on New Providence Island, required a chart and a guidebook to lead you through a few shallow spots. Athol Island is a long rugged affair used by the locals to dump anything metal into the sea. The shoreline is covered with old barges, tugboats, sunken ferryboats, and the cast-off refrigerators and other appliances no longer functioning. The next island was Paradise Island, named by Merv Griffin and built to serve the gambling public after Cuba kicked the mob and the capitalists out. No garbage there.

The yacht clubs and docks were to our left, so we eased over in that direction. I anchored off the largest pile of conch shells I had ever seen and scrambled ashore for a look-see. There were enough conch shells on the shore to give, one each, to every visitor in Disney World for the next hundred years. My tattered Top-Siders were put to the test getting through the seaward tumbling shells. By the time we got to hard ground, our hands and knees were scuffed and battered.

The first local to pass by, as we hit the pavement, looked our way and said, "Coke or smoke?"

For the uninitiated, coke is cocaine, and smoke is pot. I told him we were more interested in peanut butter and beer. He walked on in disgust. His product was not our product. A familiar face beamed from a red-and-white sign propped in front of a small restaurant. Yes, it was the colonel, and we were ready for chicken. I noticed a real stuffed chicken in a glass box designed to test the skill of a game player while attempting to snag a plastic egg with a prize inside. It was the worst-looking stuffed chicken I had ever seen. On the other hand, our expectations of having a typical fast-food meal were dashed when I noticed a larger-than-life native woman wielding a large cast-iron frying pan full of hand-floured chicken parts slowly frying the good old-fashioned way. The sides were peas and rice and fried plantains. We were in heaven; the chicken in the game machine was pitiful, but the unexpected meal was great.

Our next stop was the telecommunications building on Bay Street, right in the middle of town. Nassau had lost its luster since the departure of the British. It had slipped, just slightly, into the third world. To make a phone call required an interview by a young lady at a desk to convey the phone number. You then took a seat and waited until the international operator connected the call. You were then assigned a phone booth and requested to deposit $7 in quarters into the phone slot. It beat the heck out of writing a letter, sealing it with wax and an imprint from your ring, and then placing it into the hands of a schooner captain bound in the direction of the recipient. Of course, that could take months or years. The third-world phone was much faster. Did I mention it was ninety degrees in the phone office?

Frankie picked up on the third ring.

"Where are you?"

"We are in Nassau. I guess that is about three days from Miami. How have you been?"

"I'm teaching ESL to the Cubans coming over from Mariel, Cuba. It's a good job, and they are desperate for bilingual Spanish speakers."

"I gave Calvin your phone number in case Hugo ever shows. I doubt he ever will. I think he must be mixed up with the guys in Okeechobee."

The operator started squawking about more money in the phone. I told Frankie that I loved her and would be in touch in a week or so. Danny was on the curb outside with a cool Bahamian beer in his hands. Beer is always better with conch fritters, so we headed for the Poop Deck for happy hour, $2 beers, and free fritters.

The weather was a little feisty, northeast twenty-five knots, so our trip to the Berry Islands would be fast and furious. The entrance channel to Nassau Harbour is short, with the sea buoy just a few hundred yards from the end of the jetty. Two hundred feet past the buoy, the bottom drops to twelve thousand feet really quick. Northwest channel is open to the northeast as you leave New Providence.

Fortunella rode the first ten swells nicely until we reached the really big ones. We turned to the west, put the waves and the wind on our starboard quarter, and watched the knot meter head for nine. The quartering seas were ten to fifteen feet and pushing us hard in the right direction.

We slid around Whale Cay, thirty-five miles from Nassau, in four hours. A fleet of charter sailboats was anchored in the harbor at Chub Cay. It was a little crowded for all the boats, so we anchored outside in an open roadstead. As soon as the hook was in, we both jumped overboard and swam to the closest boat in the hopes of an invitation for dinner. Sure enough, we were invited on board for hors d'oeuvres and beer with a boatload of tourists, from Florida mostly, diving and enjoying the sun and scenery. Danny and I certainly enjoyed the scenery while the captain/guide served us cheese plates with chunks of lobster and conch.

I kinda liked what was happening on that big old charter boat. It looked like a future for *Fortunella* and me. The charter boat was about sixty-five feet long, with a single rather short mast. The interior was white-painted plywood with lots of bunks and curtains. The galley was a two-burner propane cooker and a sink. They must have eaten a lot of sandwiches. *Fortunella* was a much smaller vessel. The rich teak decks and interior, varnished cabin sole and furniture, made it beautiful but not very practical as a large group charter boat, but what did I know? This charter dream nested firmly in my frontal lobe as I slowly backstroked my way home for the evening.

Danny and I raised anchor before sunrise, eased out past Mama Rhoda Rock into deep water, and brought the bow to 270 degrees. We sailed in the abyss for three hours to Northwest Channel Light. The bottom changed from nine thousand feet to fifty feet in a thousand yards. Below we could see massive coral heads, so it was time to fish again. Danny had just poured a can of Dinty Moore beef stew into a pot when the fishing line streamed out. I ran to the stern and hauled in a magnificent yellowtail snapper. Danny took one look at the fish and dropped into the galley to retrieve the soup and chuck it overboard. We had eaten enough canned stew.

Russell Beacon was way off to our left and marked the mid-point of our passage across the Bahama Banks. The water was about ten feet deep most of the way across the bank. As we glided through the crystal-clear water, we could see every sea fan, coral head, conch, and wandering nurse shark. I was hypnotized by the view. The small string of islands known as the Biminis emerged from the horizon and grew slowly larger.

The island called Bimini has a whopping big radio tower that any sighted human can see miles away. I adjusted our course to the south, about ten degrees, to make our landfall on the east side of Gun Cay, about five miles south of Bimini. The deep passage west to Miami was through a narrow slot between Gun Cay and Cat Cay. Late in the afternoon, the wind had risen to a small gale right on our port quarter, meaning the east side of the island was going to be damn rough if we planned to anchor. Our increased speed brought us to the back side of the island just before sunset. The little drawing in the guide showed the route around the very tip of the island. The instructions cautioned to stay an arm's length from the rocks. It then advised to stay just outside the breakers, crashing onto the cliff, and continue until the lighthouse was due east of your vessel. A ninety-degree turn to the west was advised before continuing off soundings. This all seemed fairly simple, so I proceeded to hug the rocks while Danny kept warning of imminent destruction. Fortunately, the island gave us a lee from the thirty knots of wind from the east, so we were spared the crashing surf. It was an opportunity to drop our anchor in twenty feet of water and enjoy the relative peace of the lee. The anchor hit the water just as the sun sank into the sea. The plan was to have a simple meal, sleep for a while, and rise at midnight, haul anchor, and head for Miami.

Two hours into our slumber, the cabin around me started to heave violently. Bracing on the cabin walls, I pushed up through the hatch and ran into Danny, already in the cockpit. I had felt confident that the easterly wind would hold us off the island, and if we did drag anchor, it would be off to the west into very deep water. The wind had a different plan. Pulling around to the southwest, the wind was now pushing us toward the hard vertical side of the island. With no time to spare, Danny ran forward to retrieve the anchor chain. I fumbled with the wires hanging from a wire harness in the cabin. The key mechanism had some serious corrosion issues, so I had to hot-wire the boat every time we wanted to start the engine. This procedure took a few seconds. When all the sparking was over, and the starter motor successfully started the engine, Danny was on the bow yelling about imminent danger again. It was so dark I could only see the white surf as it crashed into the dark cliff.

How could the waves get so big so fast? I thought. Glancing at the fathometer blinking ten feet, I hauled the helm over and turned the boat around to a heading of 270 degrees. The waves rolled down the deck and up onto the windshield, obscuring what little vision I had. The tachometer needle hung on 2,200 rpm; the numbers turned red after that. In a few minutes, we had crossed into the deep water between Florida and the Bahama Banks. This chasm called the Florida Straits was created 250 million years ago, at the beginning of the Mesozoic Era. The African continent decided to waltz off to the east and have a little time on its own. It left a lot of torn crust behind.

Fortunella was now plunging through twelve-foot seas. The blessing was the current, and the wind was traveling in the same direction. Closing in on Miami gave us a lee shore again, if we could just survive forty miles of twelve-foot seas. The glow of Miami showed like a beacon off our starboard bow. We hoisted a reefed main and the storm jib. It was our last jib, so it had to hold together for a little while longer. The northbound current of the Gulf Stream set us hard to the right. Our course was 17 degrees south of the rhumb line to accommodate the current. The heading of 253 degrees put us high into the south-southwest wind. I sailed hard on the wind until sunrise. We were well up the coast when the sun emerged from the sea again. We passed a large head boat with a crowd of weekend fisherman plumbing the depths for snapper. I got on the radio and asked the captain how far up the beach we were from the Government Cut. He laughed and told me about fifteen miles. He chuckled and advised that we get inshore enough to see the girls in their bikinis so we would stay out of the northbound current. Danny gave him a thumbs-up and asked me for the binoculars.

It was a very pleasant motor sail back down to Government Cut, along fifteen miles of condos and white-sand beaches and bikinis.

Fortunella and its crew would be a mass of tangles for the bureaucrats, housed in a brick file cabinet at the mouth of the Miami River. I had no idea what Danny's paperwork looked like, but I knew the boat's paperwork was a little sketchy.

I was too tired to attempt running that gauntlet before getting some sleep, so I headed for Coconut Grove. We hauled up in the south anchorage, secured the vessel to the bottom, and fell into our bunks. Sleep after lots of motion and stress is deep and very satisfying. In fact, it is a great reward at the end of a long journey. The boat slowly danced on its anchor while the sun moved from one porthole to another, dancing sunbeams across my face. I sprawled across the big aft bunk dreaming and sweating in the late afternoon heat. The Bahamas is much cooler because there is less land to heat up in the tropical sun. Miami, on the other hand, is hot and humid by mid-May, a harsh reality to a boater with no AC or functioning generator. Each time the boat slowly rolled to the ever-present swell in the bay, I would slide one way, then the other, in a pool of my own sweat, lubricating the brown Naugahyde covers on the bunks. That was enough.

I rolled into the cockpit to catch a little breeze. While I gathered up my thoughts, something seemed amiss. The rubber boat, rolled up on the back deck, was no longer there. The motor was also missing from its rail mount.

I yelled down into the cabin, "Hey, Danny, are you there?"

Nothing, no sound from below. I yelled again. Still no sound. I dropped down into the main cabin and noticed the Rasta Bible lying on the chart table. Not good. The Bible was part of the Rasta dude's accoutrements left behind when the batteries went dead. I thought it was a good place to store the ship's cash. Danny thought it was a good place to remove cash. I thought Danny was a working passenger; I guess he thought he was working crew. Danny had taken the $1,000 from the *Solid Gold* guys back in Staniel Cay. The dinghy and motor were all gone, and I was a mile from shore and cold beer. No time to commiserate, so I donned a mask and snorkel, popped on flippers, stuffed a twenty in my Speedo—from my other stash—and started swimming for the Grove.

The South Anchorage was a working-class live-aboard area with a mixture of yachts and shanty boats all bobbing happily together. The water was clear and shallow with lots of interesting boat gear and wildlife at the bottom. I fetched up at the dinghy dock faster than I thought I would. It was such a pleasant swim I had not realized that I had covered a mile across the harbor. The deflated inflatable was lying at the end of the dock with all the equipment still on board. Danny was gone. Time for pizza and beer, I strolled into Coconut Grove in a red Speedo cruising for American food; no one even gave me a second look. I love the Grove. Sitting in Peacock Park with a whole pizza and a pitcher of beer, I watched the sun set on Biscayne Bay. I was finally home.

Next Stop: Key West

With Danny unexpectedly departed, it would be a bit easier to officially enter the country. I thought It would be best to go right to the customs house, with the boat, and present myself and all the paperwork I had directly to the man. In the late '70s, people went to Bimini for lunch. Leaving and returning to the country was very easy with little or no government scrutiny. My problem was the transportation I arrived on. The boat was foreign-owned and foreign-registered, which required some paperwork and fees to Uncle Sam. After a bit of a wait in line with a group of ship captains, I sat down with an agent and displayed all my letters to the Coast Guard and the permission statement from the owner to deliver the boat to Miami. The agent stamped a bunch of papers and informed me that the boat could stay in the US for six months. If I moved the vessel to another US port, I would have to clear in with customs again. That was it.

Free to wander around in my own country, I motored the boat back to the grove. I had not seen my parents in quite a while, so I decided to grab a ride on the new commuter rail to South Miami. It was a short walk from the station to the condo where I had left my pickup. The truck was sitting quietly in front of the pool, on a patch of fresh asphalt paint. How could they paint a parking lot and not move the truck? It's still a mystery. Nothing had been disturbed inside the cab. It was nice to be sitting at the wheel of the truck.

Traveling at seven miles per hour under sail was my default speed now. The thought of covering 60 miles in an hour was kind of exciting. Key in the ignition, turn to the right, the engine started, although a little noisy. The truck had been sitting for about six months. Starting was a bit of a surprise, clutch out in gear, a horrible noise from under the hood. The timing chain had broken before I got out of the parking spot. I looked at the odometer; it was sitting on 150,000 miles. The interval for chain replacement on a 1970 Toyota pickup truck was 70,000 miles. The last time I replaced it was 80,000 miles ago. I had seen a Toyota dealer less than a mile from the condo, so off I went to buy a new chain, chain cover, and tension spring. I knew this was not going to be easy. Ripping off the entire front of the truck, including the grill and hood, did not seem to bother anyone in the condo association. My little redneck job went smoothly. I was on my way home in three hours with another 70,000 miles of carefree motoring in my future. I guess sex in the pool might have raised some eyebrows, but car repair was okay.

Home was a couple of hundred miles to the northwest in a land of trailer parks and retirement communities. It was a lot quieter then Miami, tomb quiet, in fact. There was not a lot going on that did not involve shuffleboard or golf.

My dad was busy finishing "the last house he was ever going to build." My mom was just glad to see me alive; if she only knew. So I told her the story about the boat, the storm, and the drug smugglers, just to confirm that I was insane.

Ed was the master of all secondhand in his small town. The top of my list was a hard dinghy and an outboard that worked. Ed was in the Ford Country Squire chomping at the bit to scrounge a small boat and propulsion. In a town where almost everyone is over sixty, all the garage sales have sixty years of junk, and the owners are really tired of owning the junk. Within an hour, we had a skiff and a motor and were back in time for lunch.

I called to let Frankie know that I had arrived in the States and planned to bring the boat to Key West to see her. She was glad to hear that I had made the trip safely and was excited to meet me in Miami and help bring the boat to the Keys. I also spoke with friends nearby about sailing down to the Keys with Frankie and me. They were also very excited. I arrived at the boat ramp in Coconut Grove with the skiff on the top of the truck, the outboard in the back, and a six-pack on the seat. Getting the boat off the truck without help would be hard. I set the six-pack on the hood, and all the tree-dwellers descended from their nests in the fig trees and offered assistance. They are willing to work when lubricated with beer. Who says the homeless won't work? The new dinghy was a nice ride out to the boat. Just in case, I towed the old inflatable behind me. It was nice to sleep in a calm bay with no swell to rock the boat and no drug traffic to wake me up in the middle of the night.

Frankie, Steve, and Charlie (Charlene [yes, another girl with a boy's name]) all arrived the next day. I met them at the dock, and we all went to the Winn Dixie to stock the boat for the trip south. South Miami was an armed camp. There were armed troops on every corner. Smoke rose from the west end of the grove, and all the streets in that direction were blocked off. I leaned out the window to ask what's up to a guy in uniform. He told me that the blacks were rioting because the Marielitos were taking all the jobs.

"What's a Marielito?"

"They are the refugees coming from Mariel, Cuba."

"What's the deal?"

"Castro has decided to get rid of the dissidents and criminals. Nice present for South Florida, huh? Can we get to the marina? We live on a boat there."

"Yeah sure, if you live there, go ahead."

I had already brought the boat to the dock so we could get water and fuel and make provisioning easier. We secured the cars, loaded the boat, and headed down the bay. Biscayne Bay is about thirty miles long and five miles wide. The water is clear, and the fishing is good. There was a festive atmosphere on board as we sailed south heading for the Featherbed. There is a long shallow ridge of sandy mud right across the middle of the bay with a dredged channel through the middle. The channel is marked at each end. It took some attention to pilot the vessel into the channel. When we left the dock, the two dinghies were attached to the stern cleats; I hadn't looked behind the boat until I lined the boat on the range through the Featherbed Channel. When I did look back, I noticed the hard dinghy was gone.

"Damn! The first good shore boat I buy, and I lose it in the first hour of the voyage." I issued a general broadcast on the radio, but no one called back. I offered a $100 reward. "Still no call. Oh well, we still have the damn inflatable."

As we made our way down the back of the Keys, we met a constant stream of refugees heading north. Every time we passed a boat, they would yell over to us, "Miami, Miami." We would all point north in unison and then laugh. Poor Miami. All these political dissidents were the fuel for the fires of unrest in South Florida for years to come. Miami would never be the same. This was a disaster for the Carter administration and for South Florida.

We anchored in the mangroves behind Key Largo and watched the sunset on Florida Bay. I had never seen a roseate spoonbill or a great white heron in their natural habitat. We anchored right off Poor Jo Key in the Great White Heron National Wildlife Refuge. I would anchor here again many times over the next twenty years. At low tide, there were one or two inches of water under the boat. We sat very still as the tide ebbed, the keel rested into the soft mud. This was the first time since Frankie and I had first seen the boat in Provo that we could have a quiet moment aboard *Fortunella*. We all had a great meal and drank lots of rum.

Our departure was on the rising tide the next morning. We meandered down the Keys and passed under the Channel Five Bridge into the Hawk Channel on the ocean side of the Keys. The bridge height was marked at fifty-five feet on the chart. The VHF antenna on the top of the mast hit the green navigation light on the bridge, but neither broke. I did pass under that bridge at low tide the next time. Now that we were in open water, the sails went up, and away we went. The weather was very unsettled in the afternoon, which required several sail changes. The big jib was too much sail for unsteady winds, and the storm jib was too small. Danny and I had duct-taped the number 2 jib and hand sewn the torn seams while underway. We set that one since it was not going to last past this trip. All the various size jibs on the boat were hank-on. They required a human being to pull them from a large bag, snap, or hank them on the head stay, attach the halyard, and step back to the mast to hoist the sail to the top of the stay. In settled weather, this process takes ten minutes. In rough weather and choppy seas, it can take an hour.

I continued to do this routine for a decade or so after acquiring the boat. Eventually, I purchased a mechanical furling system to accomplish the sail change. It only takes a few minutes now. One furling sail can be adjusted to any wind condition. It is not as efficient as a single sail, but it is far more convenient. I had called ahead from Miami to secure a slip in Key West. The old navy submarine base had been given to the city to fashion into a yacht harbor. The fashioning had not started, so the dockage was cheap, and the showers were primitive. Vessels of every sort choked the entrance channel and harbor as we motor-sailed into our new home. The docks were three hundred feet long and twelve feet off the water; the pilings were concrete with no rub streaks. We needed a lot of fenders to keep the boat from being damaged by the unforgiving military piers. I picked a spot where the previous renter had nailed a dozen 2×8 planks longitudinally across the pilings to act as a giant ladder and fender. We lucked out this time. A couple of boaters came to take our lines and asked if we had come from Cuba. Apparently, all the traffic in the harbor was part of the massive sealift going on between Cuba and the US. Why would you come to Key West if you were not hauling Cubans? The going rate was $1,000 a head for the passage. With a big boat, one could make a lot of money in a short time.

The sub marina was a reflection of the anchorage in Miami. Every kind of boater and traveler had temporary quarters there. The greeting committee encouraged me to leave no loose gear on deck and lock all hatches when leaving the boat. That sounded like Miami also. Waterfronts are seldom safe. This became a theme over the next couple of years. The list of stolen items would fill up the next twenty pages, so I'll skip it. Every human in Key West was less evolved than a rhesus monkey. All loose items were collected each day by the local primates, sold for cash or drugs, and probably restolen from the buyer and sold for more cash and drugs. The constant arrival of fresh tourists and sailors provided new resources for thieves each day. Grouper, lobster, stone crabs, marijuana, cocaine, and refugee pay stolen from Cuban refugees fueled the economy of the Lower Keys. I called it the wild southeast or New York with palm trees.

Just outside the gate of the Truman Annex of the US Naval Base was a castle constructed completely of marijuana bales, stacked twelve feet high. A rental cop managed the construction and security around the seized evidence locker made of the evidence; only in Key West. I had sailed into an open-air asylum with drinking privileges, or in Jimmy Buffet's words, "A city so sweet that nobody cares what you do."

One block from the pot castle was the Green Parrot Bar, open twenty-three hours a day, with an hour break to hose the vomit and urine off the floor and out the door. The men's room sported a hollowed-out log mounted on an angle so the urine would run through a hole in the wall, out into the alley, and off into the gutter. This was the third world at three times the price. It felt good. As per instructions from the customs folks in Miami, I called the local customs office to report the arrival of my foreign-flagged vessel. The Key West office was stunned to hear from a US citizen actually obeying the letter of the law. They told me their plate was very full and to call back later, much later. I never called back.

Frankie had rented a small apartment on Whitehead Street, next to Truman Capote's house. There was a giant nutmeg tree (egg fruit) behind the house that shed the fruit and seed on the driveway and the porch. We made pies with the fruit and ground the seed into nutmeg powder. Nutmeg is the spice that sent dozens of European explorers off on perilous sea journeys around Africa to India, to avoid the Ottoman Empire, and to bring back something to spice up their bland diet. Columbus had nutmeg on his list of must-buy, as he searched for a shortcut to the Far East. The second-floor apartment received only enough water pressure to flush the toilet twice a day. Maybe that's why the Green Parrot just sluiced the pee right through the wall. It didn't take much water.

The water supply came from a desalinization plant right in town. It took a lot of oil to boil the seawater and turn it into drinking water. Everyone used cisterns before the plant was built. The conchs were used to water problems. The navy had its own diesel-powered water plant, so the water pressure was much better on the base than in town.

The ceiling in the shower of the apartment had a great array of tropical amphibians and reptiles. Tree frogs and geckos were better than fancy wallpaper. We had our own pest control team working 24-7. Frankie and I moved back and forth between the boat and the apartment, depending on water requirements, electrical blackouts in town, or the need to sleep in air-conditioning with no bugs. The summer was blazing hot with hordes of mosquitoes in the marina. The apartment was the better choice.

LONG HOT SUMMER

Hugo was not on the horizon. No calls, no letters, no Hugo. Several months had passed with no communications since we spoke on the phone. I had left my dad's phone number with Calvin back in Provo. It seemed apparent that he was not that concerned about the boat, or he was heading in the opposite direction. With all this in mind, I decided to kick back and enjoy the fishing and diving around the Lower Keys. Unlike the motto of the Green Parrot Bar—"see the Lower Keys on your hands and knees"—I decided to recreate sober.

Not ever being able to just kick back, I woke up early every day and set out on an adventure. Key West is situated at the junction of four channels. The nautical chart is a maze of channel and junction markers. From the east, south, southwest, northwest, and north. Moving around in a keelboat, conscious of hard-grounding, you must be sure the boat is traveling in safe water. There were coral heads outside the channel and man-made rock jetties at the end of the northwest channel. I explored every channel as far out as Boca Grande, the Marquises, and the Dry Tortugas. I dove everywhere; I anchored and explored the mangrove channels and the extensive barrier reefs.

I tell you this because the entire living reef I saw in 1980 died of coral bleaching within six years. The elkhorn and staghorn coral were magnificent and widespread. Star coral and brain coral were everywhere in deeper water and as big as glacial boulders. The variety of finfish and invertebrates would keep a field guide writer busy for years. I never dreamed that all this was so transitory. I brought students to this underwater wonderland in the 1980s to snorkel and experience all this diversity. They were as fortunate as I was; the reef is now complete devastation.

The loss of coral was not just in the Florida Keys but also worldwide. There is a recovery now occurring in the Bahamas, after twenty years of diversity loss. A combination of increased carbon dioxide in the atmosphere and increased carbonic acid in the water, increased solar radiation, and higher water temperatures are the apparent cause of coral death. The sea temperature rose an average of one degree Celsius per one thousand years over the last seven thousand years. It is now rising one degree Celsius per one hundred years. When environmental changes reach intolerable extremes, the complicated relationship between the zooxanthellic algae and the coral polyps on the living surface of the coral head breaks down. I guess when is now.

The island of Key West was a complicated cultural arrangement of local conchs, retired military, commercial fisherman, business people from all corners of the country, hippies, homeless, gays, and treasure hunters.

My morning ritual started at Shorty's, a local grit palace with lots of sausage gravy and great omelets. Coffee in hand, it was always an entertaining walk down to the commercial docks after breakfast. Lobster and stone crab boats at the smaller piers and great shrimpers by the dozens on the large docks. I stood, gazing at a thousand miles of rigging wire and halyards. A parking lot lay to my left. It was always empty, but not today. My mind struggled to interpret the tangle of wire and wood lying in the middle of the hard coral parking lot. The angles were wrong. My eye slowly followed what appeared to be a mast along to its base. The form of a deck lay tilted skyward. I walked closer and realized that a pirate ship was lying on its side with most of its sailing gear draped on the parking lot. There was a black flag hanging at eye level, with the familiar skull and crossed bones fluttering in the warm tropical breeze.

Mel Fisher, I knew him from Shorty's, was standing, hands on hips, hat on the ground, shaking his head. Mel's normal greeting was, "Today's the day."

Mel's tall ship/office had taken on water and heeled over into a parking lot for the last time. Mel referred to it as *The Galleon*.

He quipped that she was too far gone to save. She had been the centerpiece for Mel's salvage business for many years. People would go aboard, walk around, read Mel's literature about the sinking of the *Atocha*, become interested in the potential riches on board the Spanish gold ships, and buy into the venture through stock certificates. It was everything a treasure hunter needed to raise money and encourage investment. It now lay on its side in a parking lot. Today was not Mel's day. He had labored for years, researching Spanish records in Seville, and diving all over the Keys in search of the wreck. He had finally settled on Rebecca Shoals, west of the Marquesas Keys. They were within reach of Key West and shallow enough to work on with scuba gear. He cycled through hundreds of divers every year, all hoping to be there when the ship was discovered. There were weekly finds in the sands around the dive site, but the mother lode was still buried. I reached into my pocket, pulled out a crisp $5 bill, and handed it to Mel. He gladly accepted it and presented me with a stock certificate.

He straightened himself, grinned weakly, and said, "Today's the day." What an optimist.

Within five years, the wreckage of the ship was cleared, and a great condominium was built on the site. Its name was The Galleon.

The Call

Frankie had secured a job teaching English as a second language at a school less than a block away. We had all the inconvenience that the island could offer, including a phone. The water didn't run, the electricity only worked when it was not needed, and the phone was tomb silent most of the time.

Surprisingly, the phone came alive one day, so I dashed to answer it.

"Hello, Ron, it's your dad. That Hugo fella called, and he is looking for you in that place you were living down on some island."

"You mean Provo," I said.

"Yeah, he's looking for you there. I told him you would call him at the marina where you kept your boat."

"Leeward Going Through?"

"Yeah, that's the place. Somebody named Calvin gave him my number."

"Calvin comes through again," I softly said.

I took the number from Ed and sat down to contemplate my next move. If Hugo was a drug smuggler, I was bringing him right into the fold. If he was the real owner, he might just come and take his boat and leave me with nothing but a thanks. I chose to ignore the possibility that it could be a pleasant experience. My mind swirled with the minutiae of unconfirmed facts. I had loads of confusion and no confirmations. Finally, I decided to talk to a lawyer and get some outside advice. It couldn't hurt.

I called the marina in Provo, at a designated time, to talk to Hugo. He was there. Miraculously Hugo was waiting for the call. He mentioned how difficult it had been for him to sail so far north and how much longer it had taken. There was mention of many stops, many rums, and many women. He also mentioned Antigua race week. That takes a lot of time. My sympathy was with him, even if I was a little miffed by his lack of communication over a six-month period. He suggested that he might fly to Miami and meet me at the airport. I thought that was just fine. A date was set in the near future, and we left it at that. We could talk about the minutiae over a beer.

My plan was to drive to the airport in Miami and stop at a legal office in Coconut Grove on the way. I started out in my decrepit old truck and headed up the Keys. The radiator hose gave out in the middle of the Seven Mile Bridge; the engine overheated in the blistering heat. I pulled off at the Pigeon Key turnoff and scooped water out of a puddle in the road, filled the radiator, and headed for Marathon and a new hose. When I arrived in Coconut Grove, I turned into the first law office I saw. They were glad to see me and shuffled me right into a young lawyer's office. He explained how the law in Florida protected mechanics in the auto-repair business. He recommended that I disable the boat somehow and then place a lien on the value of my salvage and repair service on the boat. He told me it would stand up in state court as long as Hugo didn't steal the boat from me and take it out of the country. The other option was to go to a maritime lawyer and have a salvage lien placed on the boat. If money was a consideration, the state lien was much cheaper. I went with much cheaper. Lien in hand and $100 lighter, Frankie and I headed for the airport.

The flights from the islands were still propelled by reciprocating engines, big wings, and tail wheels. Douglas Aircraft made these planes just before and after WWII. The planes with four engines were bigger and faster than ones with two engines. The schedule changed depending on the passenger load and the plane model. I sent Frankie off to look for Hugo while I hid behind a mailbox. It seemed like a good plan at the time. My fear, if Hugo was a mob guy, he would just send some wise guys over to the arrival terminal and extinguish me. I didn't think they would suspect or recognize Frankie. I sat for an hour after the scheduled arrival of the plane. Frankie finally drifted back to my location, and we sloughed together on the wooden bench. It was beginning to look like he had missed the boat again.

Just as we were discussing our next move, a young man walked up to me and inquired, "Are you Ron?"

I just about jumped out of my skin. I said, "Yep, how did you know it was me?"

He said, "You are the only person here with boat shoes on that look like you have been on a boat." The soles of my docksiders had come adrift from the stitched uppers, and I had secured them with duct tape. This arrangement of silver tape holding my shoes together was obvious to another sailor. I asked him to show me his passport, and he did. I suggested that we have a beer. We talked for a while, and he pretty much convinced me that he was not involved in drug smuggling. Hugo was a small dark-haired man in his late twenties. His dress was European in style. Understated but the labels were handstitched and the colors muted. He spoke six languages, and his shoes were worn by the sea. He seemed like the real thing.

My plan, fueled by paranoia, involved putting Hugo in the truck blindfolded and carrying him to the marina in Key West without him knowing where we were keeping the boat. Paranoia seldom produces well-thought-out conclusions. Our conversation in the bar washed away some of the paranoia, so he was ferried to Key West with full view of the passage. I dropped Frankie at the apartment and took Hugo to the boat. The morning brought a reacquaintance of Hugo with the boat. While peering into the engine space, he mentioned that the engine was not the same one that came with the boat. That was a bit strange. There were two different engine manuals in the chart table, so I just shrugged it off. Maybe the druggies put another engine in the boat. The second manual was from an engine dealer in Fort Lauderdale as well as the new sails. This may have been part of a rehab done by the smugglers.

Hugo seemed to be a fine fellow, so we decided to make sail and see what the edge of the Gulf Stream looked like. We barked orders at each other while the boat shouldered into the building Gulf Stream swell. One thing big heavy long-keeled boats do well is push through big swells with ease. He was enjoying the hell out of the ride, and so was I. We bonded. One of the new words I learned that day was the French name for the jib.

I had gone forward to hoist the sail when Hugo yelled to me, "Put the *Faulker* up."

I was surprised to hear him swear like that and mentioned it to him when I returned to the cockpit. He laughed and explained to me that the *Faulker* was a German/French term for "the wind." That was what they called the jib. I, of course, explained that Faulker and fucker were very similar and thus the name in English was jib, to avoid confusion. Being multilingual, he agreed and apologized.

"St. Pauli Girls for all," I said. We touched bottles and forged on through the dark-blue sea.

Hugo and I spent a week messing about with the boat and exploring Key West. It was easy to see his concern about *Don Bosco*, sitting back in Provo. He was the captain, not the owner. He told me a wealthy French countess owned the vessel. She had commissioned him to sail the vessel across the Atlantic to the French West Indies. She would then visit the boat at her leisure. Hugo had promised to sell the boat for her when she tired of it. It was time to sell. He planned to bring the vessel to Miami and sell it. There were some engine and hull issues that needed to be attended to, and then the boat would be placed at a marina in Miami for sale. There was a weak promise that I could become port captain and sales rep for *Don Bosco*. We had agreed on a purchase price for *Fortunella*, but it was higher than my cash reserves could bear. He agreed to finance the unpaid balance and consider including a broker's fee, toward the balance, if I could sell the countess's boat for her. We shook on it, and we left the next day to put Hugo on the plane to Provo.

On our trip to Miami, Hugo revealed some of the history of *Fortunella III* over the previous six years. He told me that he and his dad had purchased a small fleet of Trintella's, ranging from *Fortunella I* through *VI*. They had them built in Holland and shipped to Belgium. They would then sail them to a tax-free port. The vessels were then registered in the tax haven as a corporation to avoid taxes in the future. When they were sold, the money was then deposited offshore and never returned to the country of origin for taxation. This was a quasilegal way to export money from a tax-heavy country. Everybody does it, if they are in the tax-avoidance income bracket.

Two of his boats were in Yugoslavia, two were in the south of France, and *Fortunella III* was in the Canary Islands. He had hired an out-of-work Belgian to captain and maintain *Fortunella*. Hugo would send people to the island, and Jacque would sail them around. It seemed to work well until Jacque brought up Miami as an option for the boat. Hugo explained to him that insurance for an Atlantic crossing was too expensive. Since Jacque did not own the boat, and Hugo had given him $10,000 to maintain the boat, Jacque set out for Miami.

"Rather trusting of your fellow man, aren't you?" I said.

"You have to start somewhere," Hugo remarked.

I figured Hugo had told me this story to make me feel sorry for him, or he was just a rich young guy that did not know the value of a dollar.

The statement did jive with the Coast Guard's story that Hugo contacted them about the boat being stolen. I still did not know where Hugo's point of reference was. Was he a diamond merchant, used-car salesman, social worker, or whorehouse owner? I just didn't know.

I put Hugo back on the forty-year-old Gooney Bird to Provo and headed back to Key West. It was August now. The first time I saw the boat was in January. Not to dip into my savings, I contacted an old friend who now owned a swordfishing boat. Ray and I and a college kid made a few weeklong trips up the Gulf Stream dragging fifty-two thousand feet of longline. We caught swordfish, tuna, mako sharks, and lots of other less-valuable sharks and ate cold sandwiches and pooped in a bucket for weeks at a time. We always returned smelling like dead squid and fish guts. It certainly was a high adventure, and it took my mind off the problems of the boat. I did learn that the reason you do not need a vita to commercial fish is that no one fishing has a résumé unless you include a criminal record. I seem to remember a $12 check at the end of an entire week of slogging around in the ocean, in fish guts and cold bologna sandwiches. Frankie was quite vocal about my aroma after each trip. I did try taking a bath overboard one day, but the sharks were already using the tub, so I got back on board quickly.

One day, when I smelled pretty good, I received a phone call from Hugo in Miami. It had taken him much longer than he had figured, but he was here and wanted a security deposit. He said he was going to Europe on business, so he would get all the paperwork for the boat and return posthaste. I called AG Edwards and asked for a $15,000 check to be sent to the Coconut Grove Bank, and I would pick it up as I passed through. On my way up the Keys, I spotted a hitchhiker along US 1, so I picked him up. It then occurred to me that I would be traveling with $15,000 in cash, probably in a bank bag, before I left him off. Best to deliver him first, then go to the bank. I had also called ahead to a lawyer friend and had a bill of sale drawn up with the particulars that we had agreed to for Hugo to sign.

I arrived at the bank, parked right up front, and walked right up to the front desk. I announced my name to the lady at the desk and informed her that I would like $15,000 in hundreds, please. She got up, ambled to a cash drawer, and withdrew the money and bagged it. I was ready with ID and sweaty palms when she thrust the bag in my direction and thanked me, no ID required. I blinked a few times and slid out the door.

Passing from an AC–cooled money storage box to Gulf Stream–heated Miami air immediately fogged my Foster Grants. The inside of my truck was hotter than an outbuilding on a Georgia prison farm. I was ready for a cold place and a colder beer. Hugo had put the *Don Bosco* in the downtown marina. It was hard to miss when I arrived in the parking lot. The boat had two very large wooden masts sitting on sixty-five feet of teak and oak with a waterproof bottom. Hugo and his mate were lounging on the deck. They welcomed me and offered me coffee in the largest cups I had ever seen. Hugo explained that hot beverages in the heat made the drinker cooler. I suggested we might try out that theory in the air-conditioned bar while I consumed a cold beer. He and I slipped into the cool darkness of the Chart House Bar.

Hugo was obviously from a very wealthy family. He was very concerned about the food he ate and how he was dressed. His concern came from his reaction to people constantly asking him for money if he dressed well-off. It was easier to dress down and avoid confrontation. The crew member he sailed in with was a young Mexican man. He dressed in white cotton baggy slacks and a puffy shirt. Bon Vivant came to mind; hanger-oner also came to mind. He paid for nothing and asked for much. If Hugo was a smuggler, the Mexican dandy knew it and was holding it over his head. It was perplexing that the man seemed to know little about anything, provided no service to Hugo whatsoever, and as I tumbled this over in my brain, it came to me—they were a gay couple. Sex was the missing element.

I passed the sales agreement across the table to Hugo for his signature, and a paper envelope with 150 $100 bills, part of the farm back in West Virginia. I signed my copy and Hugo's copy. He passed me my copy, and we shook hands. His plan was to return to Europe for business and then bring back the proper Builder's Certificate and other ownership papers. I took him to the airport and sent him off again. The Mexican was still on the *Don Bosco*. Hugo still hadn't learned about leaving vagrants on his boats.

Hugo flew out of the US with my $15,000 deposit, in cash in a paper bag, not exactly legal by anybody's standards.

To Document or Register, That Is the Question

E instein postulated, and then mathematically proved, that time and space were interchangeable. If you will bear with me, I will move freely around these two parameters in order to trace the contorted path I chose to legally register *Fortunella* so that I would pass muster with both the state of Florida and the US Coast Guard.

My meeting with Hugo and exchange of money and bills of sale gave me the freedom, finally, to pursue proper registration of the boat. I had been informed by the customs agent that the boat would have to be entered formally into the country once I had purchased it. Since I was in Miami, there were individuals called customs house brokers that would gather all the information about the value of the boat and its gear and submit it to the customs folks for an assessment of duty. This seemed hard and fast information that, as a novice in these circumstances, I would have to follow. After a brief interview with a broker in the port of Miami, I left thinking this was going to be a protracted and expensive process. I left the paperwork with the broker and headed back to the Keys. Not knowing what the tax-rate percentage was, I could only imagine how much the government was going to want to allow *Fortunella* to gain citizenship.

Living on the distal end of a submarine pier puts you a long way from a head and shower. I had made the trek to the head in the hot morning sun and needed a little shade before I went into the even-hotter bathroom. The city was renting the old navy buildings to local businesses, so there was always activity at this end of the pier. There was a large fellow bellowing out orders to a small gang of boat workers. They were standing on the fiberglass hull of a newly emerged-from-the-mold sports fishing yacht. Intrigued by all the activity, I made a beeline for the big guy.

"You build this boat from the resin drum to the finished boat?"

"Yup, that's what we do."

"What's the process to get them registered once they are finished?"

"Not much, you just drive up to Marathon and fill out a paper basically telling the state of Florida that you just built a boat, and you need some numbers. Pretty damn easy."

"Okay, thanks for the info."

"Pretty damn easy" was the catchphrase. Nobody but me and a few uninterested friends knew anything about *Fortunella* and her origins. Could I just register the boat with the state of Florida, pay them their fees, and go on with life? It seemed possible to me.

The next day, I was rumbling up Route 1, bound for the Florida Marine Patrol headquarters in Marathon Key. I arrived in the parking lot, killed the engine, and sat still in the blazing hot unair-conditioned truck for enough time to think about the falsehood I was about to lay on the state. Florida, being an amalgamation of humanity, just trying to make a living and stay out of the sun, would probably consider my shenanigans a positive contribution to the state coffers.

Oh hell, let's just do it, I thought. The room was air-conditioned and felt like the North Pole. I announced that my dad and I had just finished building a forty-foot sailboat and needed some numbers to stick on the bow. A woman behind the counter got up and pulled a single sheet of paper out of a file cabinet and walked over and handed it to me.

"What is the name of your boatyard?"

"White and Son," I reported.

"Just fill out the dimensions and your address, sign it, and write me a check, and you are good to go."

The sweat on my face was evaporating in the polar climate, and my nerves had settled. She said the registration would be sent to my Key West PO box. I walked out with a temporary slip and a skip in my step. I had just gone down the rabbit hole.

I now had a bill of sale and a set of numbers to put on the side window of the boat. Hugo had promised to come back soon with the necessary paperwork to pursue more legal documentation for the boat. How did I know it would be months before I would hear from Hugo? I used the boat as a recreational vessel in the Lower Keys for the summer. There were so many illegal activities going on at the time, no one cared that my paperwork was a little sketchy. This new bogus paperwork would be okay until Hugo came up with the real ownership papers.

We need to zoom forward in time a year or so and place me in a dock office in Beaufort, North Carolina, waiting for the dockmaster to give another boater paperwork to register their boat. He handed him a small blue cardboard registration form. I glanced at it and realized how simple it was to register a boat in the Carolinas.

The next thing you know, I had registered *Good Fortune* in the next state I planned to live in. Again the state was not interested in any real proof of ownership, just a signature from the present owner, and that was me. I went out and bought a set of North Carolina numbers and placed them under the Florida numbers I already had. The only difference was the North Carolina registration had all the correct serial numbers and builder information. Now I was completely legal in one state and sort of legal in another. Now I was confident that with these numbers, I could charter legally in both states without attracting the curiosity of the Coast Guard. A friend of mine had been chartering a Japanese-built boat for decades without a captain's license or federal documentation. I figured that was the norm.

Off I went advertising, making brochures, and apparently upsetting another boat carrying passengers to the Cape Lookout Lighthouse. She, the captain of the other charter boat, informed the Coast Guard that they should check me out. One day, while sailing with a professor from Raleigh and his family, the Coast Guard decided to "check me out." They tied up to *Good Fortune*, the newly christened name, boarded me, and proceeded to ask a lot of questions about licenses and documentation. I, of course, pleaded ignorance on all charges. They took my passengers off the boat and instructed me to follow them back to the base where I was to be "seized." This was not in my plan. They instructed me to tie up to the pier while they delivered my passengers to their car in Beaufort.

I knew a little about the maritime law and the government's responsibilities when you and your boat are confiscated, so I decided to call their bluff. When a seaman passed by the boat, I yelled over.

"Hey, mate, where do I plug this electrical chord in and when is lunch?"

The seaman stopped, turned, and said, "Wait one while I check with the OD."

He returned moments later. "Sir, the officer of the day has decided to release you on your own recognizance."

Well, that was not a surprise, since I knew that the government was responsible for the crew on a seized vessel. They just didn't want to buy my lunch or pay my power bill. I threw the lines off and told them I would be in Beaufort if they needed me.

When I returned to my mooring, I was a little unsettled. I felt too conspicuous, so I fished out a can of dark-blue paint from the aft locker and a brush and painted over the entire stern, including the name. This made me feel better, even if it probably wouldn't hide me from anyone. The talk around town was that I had finally gone "pirate" and revealed my true strips. A couple of days later, the coasties came back with an ultimatum for me. Stop chartering and fix the discrepancies that they had informed me about. Number 1 was to get a captain's license, and number 2, get an American-built boat or resolve the foreign-built issues with *Good Fortune*. It was time to talk to a lawyer. Specifically a maritime lawyer.

It was only a short walk down the town dock to an old yellow-painted building with a slender white shingle swinging in the southwest breeze. In black letters, it said, "Claud Wheatly Maritime Attorney." The wooden steeps up to his door were worn by the many sailors and ship captains' shoes that had climbed them to gain Mr. Wheatly Jr.'s wisdom. I was the next in line. He saw me through the glass pane and beckoned me to enter. The room was small for the desk he sat behind. Every flat surface was stacked high with yellow notepads. They were full of information.

He smiled and greeted me in pure Southern fashion. "Come on in, how are y'all doin'. I left one chair clear just for sittin'."

"I have been meaning to stop by and just introduce myself, but I just happen to have a good reason to get to know you and perhaps use your services."

He belly-laughed and encouraged me to begin my story. I spent the next hour telling the "whole story," from the conch farm to Beaufort. He loved it.

"I think we can fix this problem of yours. It might take a little time, but I'm sure it can all work out. You know, if the DEA or the Customs Service confiscates the boat for illegal cargo or nonpayment of bills or chartering without commercial documentation—that's you—then they will put the boat up for public auction. Once that happens, the title is clear of the Flag Act, and the boat can be legally documented as a commercial vessel. We just have to trump up some charges and get the Marshals Service to do their thing. The only catch would be if someone outbid you in the auction. Then you would lose your boat. The other option would be courtesy legislation. Are you a native, son?

"No, but my dad is."

"Do you plan to stay and run your business here and vote here?"

"Well, sure I vote, and if things work out, I plan to stay."

"Well then, it should work, especially since you do educational work with the boat. The entire US Congress will have to okay a bill that it will be tacked onto. Yes, federal law will exempt your foreign boat from legislation that was passed after World War I to keep the Germans from competing with our citizens in shipbuilding and coastwise commerce. The same act, called the Jones Act at the time, gives American sailors rights and privileges under the law that was gravely needed at the time."

"Wow, that was a mouthful. How do we get something like that going?"

"Just call your congressman. He is the chairman of the Congressional Committee on Maritime Affairs. He is the guy."

"This does seem to be a maritime affair."

Claud nodded. "Yup, it is an affair."

I had made a lifelong friend. It is seldom you get to meet an exceptional human being that loves his work and empathizes with others easily. He had set me on a true course and gave me the tools to accomplish my goals. As I stood at the door, about to leave, he informed me that the captain's license should be my first goal. I enrolled in a course that afternoon.

Just about the time I finished up the semester-long course at the local community college and was preparing to head south to the Keys, I received a very official-looking correspondence from the Department of Treasury. Who knew that the Coast Guard and the Department of Commerce were under the Department of Treasury? They decided to pinch me a little by sending me a fine of $5,000 for carrying passengers on a boat not registered with them.

"Damn, you have got to be kidding me," was my first reaction. My second reaction was to get into my old AMC Hornet, recently purchased, and head up to Portsmouth, Virginia, for a confab with the first ranking Coast Guard officer I could find. The entire coast guard operation was located on the Portsmouth waterfront. I parked the Hornet in a visitor's space and breached the front door. Clutching the DOT paperwork in my left hand, I hit the inner door and walked straight by all the clerks with the attitude that the first door in the building that announced the presence of a captain behind it would be my beachhead. Four stars on the door brought my free right hand down hard on the solid oak door.

"Come in." That was a great start.

"Good afternoon, my name is Ron White, and I have come up here from Beaufort, North Carolina, to pay this fine personally and then sail down to Miami to sell my former-drug-smuggling sailboat to the first Mafia drug smuggler I can find."

Silence.

Then—"Whoa, why don't you come on in and have a seat and let me take a look at that paperwork."

It worked—no scheduled appointments, no subordinate officers, no "We will take your check and contact you later." My new friend was ready to listen to all I had to say and more.

"So your boat was a drug smuggler."

"Miami to the Dominican Republic for probably three years. Dropped off in Provo with a leaky exhaust system. I watched it for a while and then pursued the owner and actually found him after a long search. I was working as the manager of a research and educational foundation on a small island near Provo. The boat was just what I had been looking for, so I pursued it all the way to Europe."

"Sounds like a great story, tell me more."

I had him. I regaled him with the saga for the next hour. He had been stationed in South Caicos during his career and had fond memories of the land and the people. We had bonded. The threat to sell the boat back into the drug trade was a stroke of blind genius. I informed him that I had a brand-new motorboat operator's license. We were good.

"I tell you what, why don't we mitigate that fine down to $100 and help you get that drug boat documented."

"Sounds great."

He explained that the boat needed to be documented for pleasure and registry and that, in time, I could get *coastwise* added after some congressional legalization. This is what my friend Claud had told me back in Beaufort.

The documentation process required ownership paperwork and an unbroken chain of owners—all American—and an official measurement done by a professional. I knew there was no way to document the boat as a foreign boat, so I had registered the boat as a US–built boat and had gone so far as to have a professional measurer drive down from Miami to figure the net and gross tonnage of the vessel. All I had to do was sign the government document, which warned of severe penalties for supplying false information. Pen in hand, and sweating in the hot humid tropical air, I put the pen down and walked away from the lie. I needed to do this right. Hence the new North Carolina registration with the truth printed in indelible ink on the little blue card.

Knowing that I could take the North Carolina registration, which did not include a title, and take it back to Florida and register the boat again with a North Carolina address, I could get a new Florida title with the correct history and serial numbers. This would allow me to present valid ownership information and get another professional measurer to come to the boat, from a great distance away, and measure the boat as a different boat again. It did not hurt that my mom, Pat, was the person at the town hall that took my application for my new legal Florida title. Are you confused yet?

Measured and signed, this time I took my documentation package to Norfolk, Virginia, where teams of civil service workers sat in a large room documenting the thousands of plastic yachts that were flooding onto the market at the beginning of the 1980s. Wood was dead, and plastic would last forever. The chalkboard on the wall announced the month and year that the teeming masses of workers had managed to document. The date was fourteen months in the past. That meant I had to wait fourteen months until they would even look at my case.

I went and got a cup of coffee. *Would this ever end?* was the question sloshing around in my brain. I had spoken to a guy one day that told me that he had chartered his foreign-built boat in New York City for years without any problems. *How could that be true?* I pondered over my now-cold coffee. I fished his business card out of my wallet and called him.

He answered right away, and after I pounded him with a myriad of questions, he just said, "I will send you the letter."

"What letter?" I cajoled.

"The letter from the Cunard Lines that revealed to me how they operated a huge cruise ship in and out of New York Harbor with the blessings of the Department of Treasury. The letter is the key."

A week later, the letter showed up at my PO box. There it was, the word trick that made it all legal, "Any vessel, foreign or domestic, may leave a US port, gain the High Seas and return to the same port on a trip to nowhere without coastwise designation." That meant I could take people sailing out the inlet anywhere and go nowhere without breaking any US laws. All I had to do is document *Good Fortune* as a pleasure boat and registry, which allowed me to participate in foreign commerce and "trips to nowhere."

This did not solve the fourteen-month waiting time, so I decided to go back upstairs and recover my paperwork and carry it down to Miami. Two months later, I was standing in front of a coast guard lieutenant being reassured that since I was documenting a commercial vessel—that's the registry part—it would go to the top of the stack and be done in ten days. These were little things that the civil servants in Norfolk did not bother to tell me. This all happened in the 1980s. By the mid-1990s, legislators had tired of yacht owners petitioning them for legislation to get around the Jones Act and the Flag Act, so they changed the wording from "vessels" to "vessels over 65 feet." The 1920s were over.

All the intimidating boardings by the DEA, US Customs Service, and the Coast Guard, with the immediate question as they gained my side deck, "Is this a charter boat?" like I was public enemy number 1, like all these agencies had nothing else to do, up and down the entire East Coast than to chase an itinerant school teacher chartering a former drug-smuggling boat to people that were paying him to teach them a little marine biology. Really! Is that what they were getting paid for? As recently as 2010, a boarding party told me I couldn't charter a foreign-built boat. I immediately informed him that they had changed the law twenty years ago. He was surprised. They must have thought that the Code of Federal Regulations (CFR) is as unchangeable as the King James Version of the Bible.

Thirty-six years later and fifty thousand passengers later, I have made just a little more with the boat than the drug smugglers probably made but with a lot more hassle. No wonder people work on the wrong side of the law; there is a lot less bureaucracy.

MY NAME IS JUAN

It had been my habit to take breakfast at Shorty's most days while I was in Key West. While I sat anticipating the arrival of my huevos rancheros, I noticed the front page of the *Miami Herald* was sporting a picture of a large sailboat lying on somebody's beach. Always interested in things nautical, I read until I came to the name Hugo Bremer. Yup, it was Hugo's big new boat parked sideways on some millionaire's beach in Fort Lauderdale. The article explained that a crew member had fallen asleep while "standing off" of the inlet, and the vessel had washed ashore. The Mexican was still in Hugo's employ. I decided to drive up to Fort Lauderdale and see if I could find the boat.

The largest travel lift in Broward County was River Bend Marina. When I drove through the gate, the first two boats I saw were *Don Bosco* and *Remember*, the vessel in the news article. I checked with the office and was informed that the owner of both vessels had left for Europe, and the yard was tasked to repair *Remember* and do major repairs on *Don Bosco*. This was par for the course, so I went back to Key West and resumed my life, waiting for Hugo to call again. On the way back, I stopped at the Miami Marina to check out a hunch I had. I asked the person at the marina desk if they had a rental card for *Fortunella*. She confirmed that they had a card in the file that dated back two years, with Roger Pigeon signing as the captain. The coast guard base was less than a mile from the marina. I guess they didn't look very hard for the boat after Hugo reported it stolen. The Coconut Grove Marina had a similar card for the boat, leaving me to the conclusion that nobody was looking hard for drug boats or stolen boats.

When I got back to Key West, there were lots of winter tourists pouring into town and only a few charter boats, so I decided to get on with my life and start a little business. I made a few contacts with the largest hotels on the island. The other charter boats were smaller and carried a lot of passengers. Without coast guard certification to carry more than six passengers, I was a true charter boat, not a head boat. I also offered an educational experience aboard *Good Fortune*, the new name for the boat.

Chuck and I had come up with an idea to combine adventure with education. It worked well on the island, and I was motivated to try it with a less-exclusive public and see if it would work. My first brochure had a black-and-white picture, taken by a friend, with verbiage about the "delicate balance between the coral reef and the grass flats." The local smugglers and hucksters thought I was a mental case. Why would you mess with biology when you could run to Colombia and bring back a load of drugs worth a fortune? We were not on the same page. I got a chance many times to look at their playbook and leaf through the pages. It just wasn't my textbook.

While sitting in a doughnut shop, an old sunburned guy on the next stool advised me, "It might be a feather in your cap if you joined the local charter boat association."

I, of course, ignored him. Old guys always know more than young guys. They have the scar tissue to prove it. If I had done what he said, it might have made a difference; but in hindsight, it probably would not have. In the next month, after I unceremoniously announced to Key West that I was offering sail charters to the vacationing public, every poster and brochure I put out was stolen, destroyed, or just thrown away. This was the beginning of a campaign to discourage me from chartering the *Good Fortune* in Key West. The anonymous villain or villains preyed on the boat and me for months. It had not occurred to me that others would take such offense to my little junior chamber of commerce adventure. In addition to stealing my advertising, the very expensive gear not firmly attached to the boat was also disappearing at an alarming rate. I sailed to the reef with six paying passengers one beautiful sunny day. When we arrived at the reef, I sauntered forward to launch the new anchor I had just purchased. Just the shackle and the locking pin were on the deck. The anchor was gone. Someone had slipped into the marina during the night, in a small boat, and taken the anchor right off the bow of the boat. Without an anchor, I had to dive down and tie the boat to a piece of wreckage on the bottom. This really got my attention. Theft was a way of life in town. Bicycles, mopeds, or anything just left lying around was stolen without regret. At that point in time, I just thought I was a victim of the culture. Paranoia was everywhere. The smugglers and boat operators were paranoid of the new guy in town—me—and I was paranoid of all of them. I called it niche envy. The boat had been broken into so many times I finally had a sign made that announced to the potential burglar, "It is illegal to break and enter. It is also illegal to rig a shotgun behind the door. I have made my decision." A skull and crossbones were situated in the middle of the sign. No one ever broke in after that. To keep from shooting myself, I never attached the string to the trigger of the shotgun, just to the door handle of the head.

When you offer a boat for charter, business is much better if the prospective clients can see the boat. With this in mind, I started the great shuffle. Key West had a large number of boats and relatively small number of slips for yachts. In a desperate effort to find a slip, I went over to the Singleton's fishing fleet docks in the hopes of finding a slip near the public view. Mr. Singleton himself agreed to see me, so I asked him if it would be possible to tie my boat up on the edge of one of his docks near a restaurant.

He laughed loudly at the thought and exclaimed in a loud voice, "Boy, shrimp boats and sailboats don't mix." That was a big no.

I kept looking along the waterfront for another spot. Every potential slip I looked at had vertical concrete sides, with swell from either the Atlantic or the Gulf of Mexico punching the seawall every four seconds. This was not good for sleeping or boarding.

One night, after an extended happy hour at the Green Parrot, I returned to the boat with a friend, hoping to board the boat and have a few more drinks. When we attempted to board the boat, the friend missed the heaving rail and went overboard, hitting her head on the rail as she splashed into the deep dark water. I immediately jumped into the water and started flailing my arms about under the boat. My fingers just touched the top of her head, enough to get a handful of hair. I hauled her to the surface and managed to climb onto the dive platform with her. She was bleeding from the back of her head, so it was off to the emergency room with her strapped on my back. I only had a moped, so she had to ride like a backpack through the dark streets of Key West.

My next attempt at a public dock was just north of the submarine base marina at the customs house dock. The facility was designed for large vessels. There was a concrete mole about fifty feet from the pier positioned to hold a vessel off the concrete dock. Using the skiff, I fastened a one-inch line to the massive cleat on the mole. I then brought *Good fortune* onto the side of the pier and sprung her off with the line I had attached to the spring cleat. When I tried to get off the boat onto the dock, I realized the surge from boat traffic and the ocean were just too severe to remain there. As I was making that decision, a large red inflatable roared up to the dock with four large young men. They jumped up on the pier and sauntered down my way and took a pirate stance next to *Good Fortune*.

"*The James Bay* is coming into this slip, and you have to leave right now."

Damn, I thought, *this is getting old. I had secured permission to stay here from the owner*, I thought. Now I'm being kicked out again. I reached over to the instrument panel and removed the keys to the ignition.

"If you get on this boat, I'm dropping the keys overboard. How big is the boat you are bringing in?" Thinking both boats might stay there.

"One hundred and sixty-five feet." Barked the largest of the Speedo-clad guys.

That was a big boat; it would take up the entire pier. I softened my approach with congenial banter about the mission of such a big vessel. They explained that they had been trying to salvage one of Columbus's three vessels of discovery. That piqued my interest. In a short time, I was offering all the boys beer and more conversation about their adventures.

They helped me move the boat back to the subbase for the third time. It finally occurred to me that empty slips in Key West were empty for a good reason. *The James Bay* finally tied up in the slip I vacated and was immediately seized by the Marshals Service for non-payments of debts. The owner lost the boat at a public auction. The Speedo guys lost their jobs and would occasionally come by *Good Fortune* for beer. In a rum-fueled haze, we would laugh about me threatening to throw the keys overboard many times.

After this incident, I moved the boat to another slip at the north end of Duval Street, right next to the kitchen door of the Pier House Restaurant. It was a great spot because all the leftover food from the kitchen came my way at the end of the day. The bad thing was that every vagrant form of humanity walked by and either stole something off the boat, threw their trash on it, or just admired it. It was a busy place.

The small boat basin was now hosting three small charter businesses. Don Lang was offering snorkel trips and scooter rentals. His empire was spread around town, renting bikes and mopeds and brokering his snorkeling tours. He had come from New York with the attendant street smarts and zeal to succeed. The other business was a small charter sailboat with another New Yorker at the helm. Ken had a very good-looking girlfriend peddling, literally and figuratively, his tours from the seat of a bicycle. I was definitely the interloper of the day. I was sitting on the back deck sipping a café con leche when I noticed some uniformed activity on the pier where the other sailboat was tied up. Ken, the boat captain, was being escorted down the dock in handcuffs. Don was gesticulating in his direction with what seemed to be incriminations against Captain Ken. I hopped off my boat and moved close enough to hear Don's words as he barked in New York fashion, at the officials that now had total possession of Captain Ken. It appeared that Don had reported Captain Ken for serving alcohol to the public without a license. The ABC folks apparently frowned on such behavior. I later found out that Ken had used the term *included* instead of *complimentary* in his advertising. This made the beer and wine paid for in advance, with the charter fee.

This was the height of commercial nit-picking, but it did illustrate how savagely competitive chartering was in Key West.

One of my first charters came to me from the Pier House Hotel. The three couples wanted to sail out to a reef, eat lunch, and snorkel for a while. I suggested they order from the kitchen, which would just pass the food out the side door into my waiting hands. We got underway at about 10:00 a.m. and motored out of the harbor into the Hawk Channel. There was little wind, so I kept the engine on to maintain headway against the incoming tide. About two miles out, one of my passengers mentioned that we might have lost the Boston Whaler we were towing. I looked back, and sure enough, my dink was two hundred yards back and adrift. I put the helm down and headed back to retrieve the boat.

A black two-seater go-fast boat raced up to the dink and retrieved the bowline. My charter was now standing on the foredeck waving to the black boat. As I raised my binoculars to view what was going on, I noticed that the gentleman, now towing my skiff away, was instructing us in sign language to *fuck off*. This was dinghy number 2, this year and fairly new to me, so I went down below, retrieved my over-under shotgun (.30-30) and made my way up to the bow. The well-dressed member of my charter party asked me if I planned to shoot the guys running the black boat.

"No, I just plan to speak to them in their own language until they release my property."

It only took two shots across the bow of the pirate vessel before they released my property and scurried off like rats running from a fire. The charter asked me if this was planned entertainment. I just laughed. My heart was still pounding too hard to explain the theft problem in Key West. We had a great lunch and spent a couple of hours hanging weightless in the gin-clear water viewing the magnificent coral formations. We hauled the anchor and headed back to Key West with a load of empty beer cans and lots of tongue-in-cheek questions about the choreography of our earlier dinghy theft.

About halfway back, I glanced astern and noticed a large sport fisherman tracking right behind me. There were several men on the flybridge staring very intently at *Good Fortune* and all the passengers.

This may have been an overreaction on my part, but it seemed like the thing to do at the time. I passed the helm to one of the now-very-drunk passengers and headed down below to get the gun again. This time, I unscrewed one of the large portholes in the stern, opened it wide, and shoved the barrel of the gun out the side of the boat so the pursuing felons could see it. They immediately peeled off and headed away from our position at a fairly high rate of speed. Was this related to the incident earlier in the day, or was this a new and even more serious event? I slumped onto the bunk with the gun across my knees and tried to make sense of my day.

Meanwhile, *Good Fortune* plowed along with a completely soused helmsman directing her progress. I jerked back to reality, realized I had lost half my body weight sweating in the cabin, and moved quickly back up into the cockpit. Everyone was laughing and drinking. Not one of the six people had seen the second near disaster of the day, so I didn't have to explain any of my bizarre actions this time. Gunplay was not part of the imagined daily activities of a charter captain I had planned on. I had not shot at or even pointed a gun at anyone in my entire life, and now, in one day, I had done both. The folks got off the boat laughing and singing my praises as they staggered down the pier.

"Greatest day ever, Captain Ron." If they only knew.

While I was standing on the dock, a couple showed up from the hotel part of the Pier House and inquired about a charter. I let them know that I was available the next day, and they agreed to show up for a trip. As they departed, an elderly man parked himself on the rail and inquired about the ownership of the vessel. While I tried to think of a good answer, I inquired about his name. He replied that his name was Juan. He definitely was an immigrant with a thick accent. When I inquired about his country of origin, he told me he was a Pole. I pride myself in recognizing regional and some foreign accents, and his was not Polish. He left the accent unexplained and moved on to more disturbing questions like where did the boat come from, who owns it, and how long had I had it? I told him that I had built the boat and was just doing a little chartering while I was in the

Keys. Not exactly the truth, but I did not feel that a Polish immigrant needed to know much about my business.

The next morning, the couple showed up just as the sky opened with torrential amounts of rain. The couple joined me in the main cabin to get out of the rain. While we were enjoying coffee, they informed me that he and his girlfriend were lawyers from Miami. So we started to discuss the boat and a bit about my legal standing. Hard into the story, a voice hailed me by name from the dock. It was still pouring, so I moved quickly out into the cockpit to see who was hailing me. There was my immigrant buddy standing in the rain. I beckoned him aboard. When he landed on the teak grate, he glanced at the couple in the forward cabin. He then turned and hastened me into the aft cabin. He ducked clear of the low archway into the cabin and sat down on the bunk across from me. *This was a man who has been aboard this boat before*, I thought. It took me months to duck under that bulkhead; he already knew it was there.

The first words out of his mouth, as he settled down onto the bunk, were, "I represent a group of men in Miami that are the owners of this boat. Then he said, "This boat's name is *Fortunella*, and we would like our boat back."

He had me. The original stern board was leaning upright on the shelf directly behind me. Etched into the curved teak board was the gold-gilded name *Fortunella III*. The old man seemed a decent guy, so I spilled my guts to him. The particulars about the Mafia and sleuthing around in Okeechobee I left out, but he got the gist of the journey from the Caicos Islands to Miami with my meeting Hugo and the purchase contract. After I finished, he informed me that Mr. Bremer was in jail in Belgium. Jack Espiers, the fellow that stole the boat from the Canary Islands, had told him. I assured him that the guy I purchased the boat from had a Belgium passport with his name and picture on the document. This stopped him. I had either called his bluff, or Jack had lied to him. He feigned a laugh, then a small smile raised the corners of his mouth.

"I guess he is out of jail now."

"I hope so," I exclaimed. "I sure gave him a lot of cash and sent him off to Europe with the belief that he was who he said he was."

Juan laughed out loud and said, "I hope for your sake, he was Mr. Bremer. You will not get a refund if he is the wrong guy."

I leaned back into the seat and wiped the sweat off my forehead. Juan was hot and uncomfortable also. It was time to vacate the aft cabin, if for no other reason than to get some fresh air. As I went to stand, he put his hand on my arm. It was not a rough motion, just an effort to make me hesitate long enough to know that he was the "good guy" and that he was not finished. He then proceeded to tell me that he was not the only person from Miami attempting to contact me. In fact, the others had attempted to fly into Key West but were turned back to Miami by bad weather. Their intention was to kill me and take the boat. He had driven down with the intention of stopping them if they had landed. It seemed, at this point, that I owed him my life. I coughed up a thanks and shook his hand.

"What can I do to resolve this situation?" I asked.

He held onto my arm, looked directly at me, and told me I must go to Miami and tell my story to some of his "business associates." He cautioned me against telling the police. Bringing a gun was also not an option, a show of good faith, so to speak. He also mentioned he knew my parents' address and phone number. I'm pretty sure I had left a phone number with one of the wise guys during one of the phone calls with them when I was still trying to find the real owner.

Juan stood up and climbed up the three steps into the cockpit, turned, and handed me a piece of paper with a phone number and "Dadeland Mall" written on it. He said, "Is tomorrow good for you?"

"What time?" I asked.

"Around ten is good. Call me when you get there."

He climbed off the boat, smiled, and walked off into the pouring rain. I ducked quickly down into the forward cabin where the two lawyers were sitting at the table, drinking beer and munching on some snacks they had brought, and generally enjoying the ambiance of the boat.

I was bursting with information I needed to free myself of. The lawyers knew something was going on since I had already told them some of the story. I told them that I had just dodged a bullet, literally. They were excited by the intrigue and encouraged me to spill my guts for the second time. I told them the sequence of events up to the present. My hope was to test the legitimacy of my situation on a couple of free lawyers. Their reaction was one of amazement and excitement rather than fear and trepidation. They were more interested in hearing what was going to happen to me the next day than expressing any fear for what I was about to do.

We sat in the cabin discussing the recent events, drinking and eating while I planned the next day's journey back to Miami. I knew I was going to arrive early to scope out the mall. Not that I didn't trust Joe, or Juan, or whatever his name was, I just did not want to get caught in a cross fire in a crowded mall. No, I didn't trust my new friend from Miami, so I planned to get there early, check out all the pay phones to make sure there were no wise guys around, and then quickly make a call from outside the mall, tell Juan which phone I was at, and then sit outside and wait for him to enter the mall and go to the phone. If no one else was nearby, I would approach him.

The two lawyers wished me luck and went back to their motel room. My old rusty shotgun was calling to me from the hanging locker, so I stuffed it into a canvas laundry bag and placed it behind the front seat of my truck. The dominos were falling. I could not run fast enough to stop the cascade from falling headlong toward Miami. Convinced that even people living and working outside the law would not be interested in killing an honest guy like me, I assembled my paperwork, canceled checks, and coast guard correspondence and stuffed them in a manila envelope. I started up the pier toward the truck, and it occurred to me that this whole meeting might be a ploy to steal the boat while I was off on a wild-goose chase in Miami. The boat was secured to a navy pier with massive pilings. My thought was to run a chain around a piling and then secure it to the rudder skeg on the boat. A bronze lock joined the chain and made the boat immovable. I then turned off the fuel supply to the engine. The fuel valves were buried in the darkest corner of the engine room. Confident now that the boat was unstealable, I headed up the long torturous Route 1, back to the mainland and the Dadeland Mall.

The parking lot was empty as I rolled in and stopped in a space near enough to the southwest entrance to see the phone island inside the door. The mall had an anchor store on each end with a long corridor of shops connecting them. My plan was to check each phone in the mall to make sure I was the first to arrive and then make the call from the phone I could see from the truck. Once I made contact with Juan, I could go outside and wait to see who showed up. Equipped with a café negros and a shotgun on my lap, I hunkered down. At this moment in time, I had not made a personal assessment of my sanity. The coffee on the dashboard was strong enough to kill a lab rat; the mixture of adrenalin and testosterone running around in my brain was the only thing keeping me from bolting out of the situation and heading for the Canadian border.

The tropical sun was coaxing my sweat glands into overdrive just as a '60's vintage Dodge Dart pulled into a parking space not too far from me. There was Juan. He emerged from the car and strolled over to the entrance, pushed the door open, and walked to the phone. He stood looking around for a while and then sat down on a bench and lit a cigarette. He was air-conditioned, and I was sitting inside a one-hundred-degree tin box. It was time for me to make my move. As I passed through the glass doors with my blue laundry bag / gun case in my left hand, Juan stood up and greeted me with a big smile.

"I told you not to bring a gun. You will not need it."

My heart was halfway up my esophagus by now. I apologized to him and exclaimed that I always carried a shotgun when I was shopping. He laughed. "Let's put that thing away, and you can ride with me to my apartment for a little meeting."

He won me over without firing a single shot. He spoke to me like a good-meaning Dutch uncle. I had to trust someone in this charade, and I had chosen Juan. I got into the passenger side of his car, thinking, *If this guy is really a big mob boss, why is he driving a rusty old compact car built in the early '60s?*

We rode a couple of miles north on US 1 and turned into a small cluster of apartments. We went to a second-floor apartment with a small balcony off the living area. He asked if I cared for a drink and then scoured the kitchen for some bottled water. It was not his place. Just as we got comfortable at the table, the door swung open, and in came three men that were familiar to me. These guys were at the marina in Provo, sometime before I moved on to the boat. They were not smiling. Juan introduced them to me with fake names. I immediately recognized Roger Pigeon's voice from the phone conversations. One of the other guys had tried to charter the boat in Key West within the last week. It didn't happen because he said his child was ill, so they could not go. Juan definitely had some juice with this crowd. He controlled the conversation right from the start.

"Show them all your paperwork, Ron." He smiled again.

I spread everything out on the table for their perusal. The signed bill of sale was passed around, along with a copy of the letter Frankie and I had sent to the Coast Guard and INTERPOL. They all started to smile.

"Juan! Don't you think this guy could help us out on some of our jobs?"

"I don't think you have the retirement package I'm looking for," I said.

They all chuckled and stirred in their seats. Juan looked hard at me and said, "Do you know anything about our organization?"

I smiled the biggest grin I could manage and said, "I'm a live-and-let-live kinda guy. What you do is no concern of mine."

This seemed to make them all happy. Juan explained to me that they had used the boat for vacation trips to the islands. In fact, they had used it so much that they had to put a new engine and a set of sails on it just recently. I told him about the storm on the way north and the poor condition of the engine and sails. He hinted that it would be great if I would reimburse them for the sails and engine. Backpedaling, I assured him that I had spent all my available money on the purchase of the boat and would be in debt to Hugo for years to come. Juan mentioned that the old engine of the boat was in his backyard, with a hole in the side of the block. That explained why Hugo had remarked that the engine color was not the same. It wasn't the same engine. Juan said that an oil-cooling line had ruptured underway, and the engine ran out of oil. No wonder they had to replace it.

His eyes narrowed as he informed me that an insurance man from Europe had come looking for the boat. A cold shiver ran down my back as I mentally tried to maneuver my mouth into a position to talk. I knew that what he just said could be a lie. He was no stranger to bluffing. Did I just pay Hugo, in large bills, for a boat that belonged to an insurance company while Hugo had banked the insurance payoff as well? Did the insurance company show up in Miami to ask the Mafia where their boat was, or did they just ask a dockmaster about the boat, and he passed that inquiry on to Juan? Holy shit. Juan had just planted a huge seed of doubt in my frontal lobe. While that seed was taking root, other lower-functioning portions of my brain were placing my fight-or-flight gears into drive. My foot was still on the brake as my visual cortex was working on an escape route. Juan noticed the sweat erupting on my forehead.

He moved close to me and said very clearly, "Look, I'm a very powerful man here, and when I say it's all over, it's all over. Go back, go to sleep, don't worry about this anymore. It's all over with. Here is my phone number. We can charter the boat and work off some of those repair cost you owe us."

"Oh, okay that sounds good. Call me anytime, you have my number, and you know how to find me."

This time everyone laughed. All three of the wise guys pushed back their chairs, stood up, and stretched a little. By the time Juan was standing, the three men were at the door. Juan followed them out the door and closed it behind him. There I was, in a strange condo in South Miami, with four mob guys outside in the parking lot. All that adrenalin I had banked for the "flight" portion of my day was standing by. My brain instantly informed me that the chances of getting shot on the landing outside the door were above average. My visual cortex had already located an escape route, which was through the sliding glass doors onto the balcony and, hopefully, down a drainpipe to the courtyard below. One sweep of my hand gathered my paperwork into my shirt. A trellis of bougainvillea was my ladder to the ground. Over a small privacy wall and out onto A1A South, I trotted along singing a Jackson Brown song in my head. "I'm running down the road trying to loosen my load. I've got four Mafia wise guys on my mind."

Nothing like running down the road at midday in South Florida to get rid of some unwanted adrenalin and clear your mind for just a moment. It occurred to me that the reason I was still alive was that they thought I might be a DEA agent. That would explain all the niceties and me still living.

South Miami was my hood. The PRIDE condo was just behind the mall where my truck had been stored. The distance to each was about the same. The condo would be a great hideout, but I would have no way to get to my car if they staked out the truck. *I'm going for the truck*, I thought. Once I'm on the road, it will be Key West or bust. A taxi was sitting at a stoplight as I ran in place, waiting for the light. It occurred to me that the taxi would get me there in no time, so I jumped in and yelled, "Take me to the mall."

I had removed the old plastic Toyota grill from the truck when I rehabbed it. The truck now sported a nice varnished piece of chestnut with a sperm whale carved out of the middle, allowing less air to interface with the radiator than the original louvered plastic grill. As soon as the taxi pulled abeam of the truck, I jumped out, threw a twenty at the driver, and quickly looked around in search of wise guys. The lot was clear as I ran around the front of the truck. The whale was not going to allow enough air into the radiator to cool the truck the way I planned to drive in the next two hours. Pulling the varnished grill off the truck and throwing it behind the seat got the taxi driver's attention. He started yelling at me in Spanish as I fled the parking lot and set my course for Key Wasted. I don't know if it was encouragement or derision or just another car theft in Miami.

Traffic would be light on a weekday, so I made good time and rolled into Frankie's schoolyard at about three in the afternoon. The school where Frankie taught was old with very large windows left over from the unair-conditioned past. She was a bit surprised to spot me pressed up to the bottom pane like a tree frog mouthing instructions. She opened the window, and words began to burst from my lips. The gist of the conversation was about me getting on the boat and leaving for a while. I encouraged her to not worry; I would contact her when I decide which country I would sail to. Yes, it was a bit of an overreaction. I knew that staying in town was not an option, for the immediate future anyway. If I got underway on the boat, I would sleep better, and it would give me the time to reason out the last few days without the interruption of a gang of wise guys showing up for a party.

I stopped at the apartment and grabbed my seabag. When I turned on to Roosevelt Boulevard, I spotted a guy on a bike, and he looked familiar. He came to the truck as I rolled down the window.

"Hello, Captain. What are you up to?"

"I'm heading offshore for a little adventure. Would you like to come along?"

By now I had remembered this guy called himself Alabama. He seemed smart, resourceful, and self-supporting. I think he told me he was a contractor from Alabama.

"Hail yas—that's Southern for hell yes—I would love to go. When?"

"As soon as our seabags hit the deck, hop in, and we can swing by and pick up your gear."

The chain was still wrapped around the keel just like I left it. We cleared the chain, climbed aboard, and backed out of the slip. We needed ice and fuel, so our next stop was the fuel dock at Singleton's. A sunburned fellow with lots of infant skin cancer patches all over his arms took our lines and asked me what we needed.

"Fuel and a block of ice," I reported.

He handed me a four-inch vinyl hose and sauntered down the one hundred feet of dock. "The ice will be here directly," he said as he walked away.

I heard a big motor start down at the other end of the hose I was holding. A small roar started to emerge from the mouth of the hose. Moments later, massive amounts of shaved ice began pouring out of the hose and geysered into the air. Alabama grabbed the hose with me, and we managed to direct the ice into the icebox. When it was full, we just filled the five-foot-by-eight-foot cockpit of the boat slam full and more. It was ninety degrees everywhere but in the boat. Alabama grabbed a six-pack and shoved it into the mountain of ice we were standing in.

The dock guy looked down into the boat and said, "Is that enough?"

"How much does a block weigh?" I said.

"Three hundred pounds, Captain." That's when I learned that a block of ice to a shrimp boat was 290 lbs. more than a block of ice to a yachtsman. The good news was that our beer would be cold for a long time for only $5.

Full of fuel, ice, food (beer), and no clue about upcoming weather, we headed out the Northwest Channel into the Gulf of Mexico. My plan was to head to Charlotte Harbor and hold up in a very remote little fish camp near my parents' house, where I had lived aboard my previous boat, *Vamos*, for three years, tucked in the mangroves. It was like Br'er Rabbit heading for the briar patch.

WHAT COLD FRONT?

Late September in South Florida is warm and humid. Alabama and I were sailing north into a big bunch of water that was only sixty feet deep. I still did not have any sophisticated navigational equipment and planned to rely on the compass, speedometer, and the fathometer. The chart showed very distinct bottom contours leading up the west coast of Florida. It seemed logical to pick the fifty-foot contour and follow it north 120 miles. On this course, a 350-degree heading would intersect Boca Grande inlet in twenty hours. There is not a lot of boat traffic in this part of the gulf, so I anticipated an easy trip just sitting at the helm and watching the sights. Our mountain of shaved ice was melting a lot faster than we expected, so we enjoyed cold drinks and cool feet while we had them.

It is very uncommon for cold fronts to make their way this far south this time of year. The wind was southeast at fifteen knots, which afforded us a splendid reach on our northward journey. Yellowtail snapper was on the menu as the sun splashed down into the gulf. The sails had to be eased to accommodate a slight southward migration of the wind. By 8:00 p.m., I had to gybe the entire boat as the wind clocked to the southwest. The wind had increased to about twenty-five knots. Mike was at the helm and struggling to hold our course because we had way too much sail up.

I decided to reduce the size of the headsail, so we luffed up; and I crawled to the bow on my hands and knees, releasing the jib halyard on my way by the mainmast. By the time I reached the bow, the big jib was half in the water, so Mike left the helm and came forward to help me. We struggled for ten minutes to heave the big wet sail into the bag it was supposed to fit in. We scurried back to the cockpit dragging the sail bag with us. It was now time to set our smallest jib on the head stay. We did the same procedure in reverse this time. The wind had headed us by now, so the waves that were pushing us along twenty minutes earlier were now climbing over the bow and dousing our navels. The wind was now hollowing from the north, causing me to alter our heading to the northwest. The small jib was pulling well, and the mizzen was happy as always. The main, on the other hand, was quivering enough to set up a high wine on the luff of the sail. We were crashing into very short steep seas with lots of water raining down on the entire forward section of the boat.

Mike slipped down below to grab some rest while I decided to look at the windward rigging before I settled into the helm seat. The starboard backstay had an insulator spliced into the wire, top and bottom, to act as an antenna for the single-sideband radio. The heavy one-by-nineteen rigging wire did not like the 360-degree turn forced onto it as it passed around the ceramic insulator. Five of the nineteen wires had given up and snapped cleanly in two. The remaining fourteen wires were holding up a six-hundred-pound mast supporting five hundred square feet of sail material pulling forty thousand pounds of boat at eight nautical miles per hour through some rather wild seas. I sat for a second and attempted to procrastinate.

The voice, that little sound in my mind's ear, said, *Do it now. Go below and move sleeping Mike—Alabama—off the bunk, rummage around in a dark locker, find the rusted wire bolts, squirt WD-40 on them, locate a socket wrench, break the nuts loose, scramble to the deck with a short piece of chain, and secure the chain to the wire above the insulator and then secure the other end of the chain to the chain plate secured to the deck.* Seemed like a lot of work. The fresh hot coffee in my hand coaxed me into action. Mike sat blurry-eyed at the end of the bunk while I pushed up the cushion and fished for the gear I needed.

The windward side of the boat was a waterfall of spray, so it took several minutes to complete the rather simple job. When I finished, I slipped into the helm seat as my left hand found the coffee cup. The coffee was cold now, but the caffeine was still necessary. A huge onrushing wave, met the bow as the boat surged forward and dramatically decelerated the entire boat, including the top of main mast. Fifty feet of leverage exerted on the backstay parted the four-teen remaining strands of the stay with a loud sharp bang.

The chain stretched tight and assumed the job of holding up the mast. Holy ship, I screamed, "The voice saved my ass again."

Mike appeared in the companionway with a puzzled look on his face.

"Are we okay?"

"We are more than okay. We are still underway, with everything still standing."

The sun slid up over the west coast of Florida and revealed a line of sugar-white beach with palm trees and the ever-present Australian pines. The sea buoy for Boca Grande was a mile off the port bow and closing. This was my briar patch, and Eldred's Marina was my rabbit hole. I knew that it would be tough to squeeze this big boat into a little fish camp, but no one would ever look for it there. We anchored off the channel, had a quiet dinner, and waited for the tide. Fortunately, the moon was full, and the highest tide of the month would be early in the morning.

At sunrise, Mike went to the bow and hauled the anchor, and I nosed the leading edge of the keel into the soft sand at the mouth of the channel. I jumped overboard and swam to the bow, found the deepest part of the channel with my feet, and guided the boat over the bar and into the small palm-fringed basin. Jim Dixon stood on the dock, with his hands on his hip boots, and just shook his head and pointed at an empty slip. Yes, it looked ridiculous to tie this forty-foot ketch to a dock made for a twenty-foot runabout, but it worked. Jim stepped onto the dock and welcomed me home. I thanked him and asked if he could keep a very close eye on the boat for a while.

He patted the .45 on his hip and said, "I'll doer."

Jim was a Tennessee mountain boy who liked his life and his privacy. Every year or so, some developer would come along and offer Jim millions of dollars to buy his marina. My mom would always send me the front-page picture in the local paper of Jim turning down another offer. Personally, I hope Jim never sells; his kids might, and that's for another time.

My dad was surprised and glad to see me. He wanted to be caught up after he had received the call from Calvin. We spent the evening catching up and making a plan for the near future. We, Mike and I, would bus back to Key West to pick up my truck, and I would head for the West Virginia mountains for a while. Mike had enough adventure with Captain Ron, so he traveled back to his car with me and thanked me for a great time. Mike was a great mate and traveling companion. I hope he is well and prospering.

HOME AMONG THE HILLS

It had been a year since my feet had been in boots, touching the red clay of the Central Appalachians. It was fall in the hardwood capital of the east. Colors dripped from the trees to the ground in yellow and red circles on the bright-green grass. Every vista gave pause for artistic reflection. Morning mist blanketed the tapestry and slowly gave way to the heat of the last summer rays. Lying in the grass, warm sun on my exposed skin, I reflected on my last year in the tropics. Sun at thirty-nine degrees north latitude was always working to get your attention, and it always felt good to the touch. The tropical sun, at twenty-three degrees north latitude, on the other hand, was a devil to be avoided. Its hot touch seared your skin and wrinkled the dermis on your nose into a crust. This easy sun felt very good, and the soft cool earth, cushioned everywhere with a moist moss carpet, felt nourishing between my bare toes.

Not much in the mountains had changed in my absence. Everyone I knew was content with his or her surroundings, still enjoying the summers and enduring the winters. The biologists I worked with at the US Fish and Wildlife Service were still slaving away on countless environmental-impact statements. I hung with my friend Mike and drifted between his couch and a tent in the woods. It was great to be anonymous and insulated from all the druggie issues of South Florida.

My dad was equipped with Mike's telephone number, and one crisp fall day, he used it. Mike took the call and the message. Hugo was on his way to Fort Lauderdale. No time of arrival, location, or intention. I called Ed and pumped him for information with little more than the original message. Reluctantly I decided to go down from the mountain, like Moses, and see what had happened since

I left the sunny south. My rusty old truck loved the trip downhill to the Piedmont and onto the emergent floodplain of Florida. I visited all the boatyards in Broward County and stopped in to see *Don Bosco*. She was hauled out, and work was in progress on the bottom. The yard manager told me that Mr. Bremer had called and ordered this work to be done. The call sheet in the office had Hugo's contact number. I went to the pay phone outside the office and punched in the number. The operator told me to deposit $8 in quarters.

"Where the heck am I calling?"

"Greece," the operator replied.

Greece again, I thought, *how many wine festivals can one guy go to?*

She put the call through, and sure enough, Hugo answered. He told me he really intended to be there, but the party was just too good to leave. He did not have the paperwork for the boat with him and planned to go to Belgium and on to Florida soon. He should be back in the States within a month. At this point, I raised the volume. I screamed into the phone that he would never see the boat again if he didn't bring the paperwork soon. I then told him about the wise guys and that I was scared shitless. I then told him they—the wise guys—had tried to kill me, and if I didn't see the papers soon, that was it. He was indignant and oblivious to my plight. I told him I was tired of the mysteries. I wanted everything on the table.

I then screamed, "These assholes have guns!" That got his attention. He then assured me the papers would be with him when he came back on the twenty-fifth of October.

It was time to return to *Good Fortune* and get on with my life. I seriously doubted that Hugo was going to show up, so I was content to keep the boat at the deposit price of $15,000 and move on until the situation resolved itself. I had agreed to pay an additional amount, financed by him, when he brought the paperwork back from Europe. He would probably not let me off the hook until he was finished with the deal.

Ed had talked up the boat at the local Moose Lodge, so there was an interesting cast of characters waiting to sail back to Key West with me. The moon was right; the wind had pushed even more water into the channel, so the departure from Eldred's Marina was quite easy. The trip back to the Keys was uneventful, and all had a splendid time with calm seas and gentle winds. Another Moosekateer drove down from Englewood to Key West and stayed on the boat while we drank large quantities of beer and rum. When the hangover cleared, we all got in his Caddy and headed back to Englewood, where I retrieved my truck again.

SAIL WITH GOOD FORTUNE
(FOR FUN AND PROFIT)

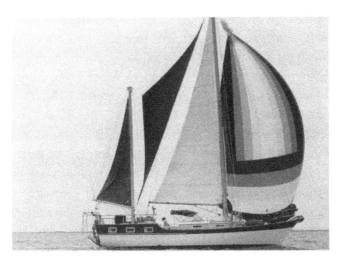

S o it was time to start chartering. I had lost Hugo for a while, and I had all the fake numbers and titles I needed for *Good Fortune* to operate in the state of Florida. The plan was to contact some of the colleges Chuck and I had hosted on the island and see if they were interested in in situ education in the Florida Keys. On the way to the Dry Tortugas, there were several small island groups with lots of grass flats and mangroves to muck around in. My alma mater was interested in a twenty-day trip in January. To make the trips afford-able and profitable, the passenger load was a total of ten people. The Coast Guard was tasked to regulate charter groups to six passengers, plus the charterer. There was so much illegal stuff going on in South Florida at the time it didn't seem like this was a serious infraction. I did all the cooking, sailing, cleaning, and repair. The congestion of that many people on the boat was very difficult. It should have been obvious that *Good Fortune* was too small for the type of business I planned, but it wasn't. I was too much in love with the boat by now to start over with a larger boat.

The first group were all exceptional students and gave me a great start in this type of educational chartering. While we were anchored in a small basin adjacent to Fort Jefferson, in the Dry Tortuga, a gale started to blow. The big anchor that came with the boat was designed for rocky bottoms in the North Sea. The bottom we were on was smooth limestone with a thin veneer of sand. There were about ten boats in the anchorage, all downwind of us. When the sun went down, everyone was worn out from the day's activities, so we turned the lights out early. I was roused by a noise from the starboard rail sounding like we were hitting a dock. When I looked out of the hatch, there was a sailboat lying on our hip.

I quietly roused the students to help me fend off the boat while I determined our next move. With the help of a spotlight, we noticed that our anchor had hooked on the anchor line of the boat behind us and had slid up the line to the bow of the boat we were now next to. The students were anxious to participate, so I instructed them to board the other boat and quietly slip forward and throw our anchor overboard, away from the other boat. They did just that and man-aged to get back aboard *Good Fortune* before the boats separated. I told the students to recover our anchor and we would use the engine to move the boat upwind again.

The other boat was full of "spring breakers." We were so quiet they never even looked out of their hatch.

It was very dark, so the only way to identify another boat was by their anchor light. As I motored into the wind, I noticed the light on the boat behind me was not getting farther away. I pushed the throttle forward, and the light behind me stayed with us. We shined the spotlight down the side of our hull and realized that we had hooked his anchor with our anchor, so we were towing him along in the dark at five knots without his knowledge or permission. No one appeared on the deck while we towed them through the anchorage. We were at least one hundred yards from where he had been anchored, so we very gently dropped his anchor overboard and stood by to make sure it hooked. Off we went to another spot and reanchored for the rest of the night. All this boat dancing in thirty knots of wind on a moonless night and without a single soul awakened. I did hear the captain of the boat we repositioned remark that he thought his boat had moved during the night. *It certainly did*, I thought, *but not by Mother Nature.*

A Pot of Trouble

I was looking for an upscale hotel in Key West to offer custom charters for the day or longer. Henry Flagler built the Flagler Hotel as
a culmination of his Overseas Railway stretching from Homestead
to Key West. One hundred and sixty miles of islands and bridges. A
hurricane destroyed the railroad in 1935. The state of Florida built a
highway on top of the tracks and bridges to reconnect Key West to
the rest of the country. After years of neglect, the hotel was rebuilt by
Marriott International and renamed The Casa Marina in 1979, and
reopened.

The water activities coordinator at the Casa Marina Hotel
called right after nine one morning to inquire if I was willing to take
a single person out for a snorkel trip.

My retort was, "How single?"

They said she looked pretty single, with an emphasis on pretty.
I told them it would be a hardship, but I would do it.

Betty was a nurse from Montreal, on a break from the snow and
ice. She met me at the sub base and looked delighted to see the boat
and me. Lines off and the sails up, even if there was no wind; all the
better to snorkel. We cleared the end of the island and headed out the
main channel toward Sand Key. It was unusual, not another boat in
sight and a calm sea. We motored along through the beautiful clear
water until I noticed a dark square object off to the southeast. The
sea is full of flotsam so it would not be unusual to see something out
on this course. This flotsam looked bale-like and floating high. The
locals call them square grouper. They are the size of a bale of hay and
weigh about one hundred pounds.

When we pulled up to it, I noticed that the plastic cover had
adult gooseneck barnacles attached to the waterline. This particular

group of barnacles is a pelagic species from the deep ocean. I was certain it was a bale of pot. My passenger, now leaning over the side with great interest, asked what it might be.

"It's a life raft without the plastic case."

I dumped the mainsheet, pulled the engine into reverse for a few seconds until the boat stopped, and jumped over the side and wrapped my arms around the mystery object. With a boatload of adrenalin, I managed to barge the package to the swim platform and up the stern ladder to the back deck. Yes, it was a hundred pounds plus. I hauled it across the deck, down the companionway into the forward head, and closed the door behind me before my passenger had a chance to make a further inquiry. I popped out of the cabin, grabbed two beers out of the cooler, handed one to Betty, and screwed up enough courage to announce, "This is your lucky day, you are now on a free charter."

She smiled and said, "Well, I guess so."

I took Betty out to the reef and showed her my underwater world. We swam among elkhorn and staghorn coral in shallow water, some breaking the surface at low tide. There is little more magnificent than the beauty of a mature reef crown. The light plays with the golden coral as the white-capped waves cruise through the massive coral slabs, as they appear to emerge from the water with the passing wave. How could we know this reef would be dead within ten years?

Warming surface temperatures are thought to affect the health of the commensal zooxanthellic alga living in and around the coral polyps. If the alga dies, the coral polyp will also die. This condition is called coral bleaching. Another condition is actually caused by divers squirting bleach into a coral head to drive the lobsters out and into their waiting hands; they are not the same. One is caused by increased seawater temperatures, killing the coral, leaving large areas of dead white coral. The other is caused by humans directly squirting bleach on the coral head to drive lobsters out into the divers' catch bag. Either scenario kills the coral!

I pulled the anchor out of the bottom, and the boat fell off to the north. The wind had picked up enough to make it challenging to hoist the main. The head of the sail peaked, and I ran back to secure the mainsheet as the boom flailed back and forth across the deck. Just as I passed the windshield, the boom lurched across and hit me in the chest and swung me overboard as I clutched the bottom of the sail. Betty had the presence of mind to grab the mainsheet and haul the boom and me back inboard to safety. Betty was a better sailor than I thought. It took a few more beers and a good sail back to the marina to get over the near-overboard incident and the recovery of one hundred pounds of pot. When we got back, I opened the bale and filled a Ziploc bag for Betty's trip back to Canada. I bet she never forgot that day, and neither will I.

Betty went home to Canada with a great story to tell her friends and left me with ninety-nine pounds of trouble. There are those who would love to have this kind of problem. Not being a serious pot smoker, it seemed the best course would be to pass the bale on to someone with a little more passion for the project than I could muster. I had done a three-day charter with a group from Boca Raton a few weeks earlier that left me with the impression that my new roommate wrapped in plastic would be a great hit with them. These folks showed up at the boat with a leather suitcase full of Jack Daniel's and quaaludes and not much else. They partied on the boat as much as people could party consuming a lot of depressants. The three days were spent mostly naked and totally stoned. When we returned to the dock, they left to return to their button-down jobs at IBM writing policy and operating manuals. With their affinity for mind-altering substances, it was a good bet they would be interested. I called Richard—pronounced the French way—and revealed to him that I was hosting a fairly large amount of pot in the forward cabin of the boat. Richard was delighted to hear this and asked me if I could drive it up to Boca.

Since my old truck was uncomfortable, hot, and undependable, I decided to rent a spankin'-new Datsun, from Avis at the airport, and proceeded to Boca. The bale fit nicely in the trunk of the compact car. What a delight to head up the Keys in an air-conditioned auto with less than three hundred thousand miles on the odometer. My mind was concentrating on my interaction with Richard, and perhaps Fish, a friend of Richards, when I spotted an ice cream shop on the east end of Big Pine Key. I swung into the lot and headed for coffee, ice cream, and air-conditioning. The TV hung down from the wall like in a hospital room, and most of the patrons were glued to the screen as I entered the cool realm of sweet smells and crisp air. The announcer was spinning a tale of a bank robbery and a fiendish getaway in a gray Chevy Nova. He said there was a roadblock at the north end of Marathon Key, so be prepared for traffic congestion on Route1. I, of course, was traveling on Route 1 north to Marathon with a trunk load of illicit cargo.

"Shit," I exclaimed out loud. Everyone in the room turned to see me in a state of emotional distress. I'm sure they thought I might be the bank robber, so I continued, "I will never make my mom's birthday party with all that traffic."

They bought it as I slinked out into the parking lot and got into my red Datsun rental car. The damp marijuana had begun to cook in the trunk of the very hot car and was emitting an odor identifiable by almost anyone within twenty feet. It was time to head back to Key West and dump the car with Avis and make a new plan. Boy, was that close.

Sears was sporting a large sign in the window when I arrived back in Key West. The sale was for large plastic trash cans guaranteed for seven years. I needed a trash can, and my pot bale needed a trash can, so I turned into Sears and bought that can. Magically the bale fit right into the can. I placed the can full of grass on the dock, taped it closed, and wrote on the tape "This is not a trash can" and called Richard. He was very reticent to come for the retrieval, so I passed this info onto an old friend who, one night, slipped onto the sub base, removed the pot, and disappeared into the night. Of course, I didn't give him all the pot, which brings me to the rest of the story.

Frankie and I had drifted apart by now. The constant stress of not knowing who any of the characters in our lives were and what their real motives were finally pushed us apart. I had started dating a waitress from the Pier House and was slowly realizing that she was dating in-gender also. For the time being, we were just having a heterosexual relationship with homosexual overtones. There were certainly several shades of white. Sara, the waitress, had introduced me to several friends who specialized in pot transportation. I visited a home in a very middle-class neighborhood that had a pot drying room rigged to wash and dry wet marijuana. The room had four dehumidifiers and a trash compactor to dry and compact the wet pot back into a dry bale. A Cadillac would arrive from Miami and transport the pot north. The rub was that the transporter required at least a trunk load in order to make the journey from Dade County to Key West. Thus, a new unit of measure was invented—the Cady trunk load. One bale was not enough. I was so glad that my friend's requirement was only a Toyota trunk load.

A girlfriend of a friend called to ask if she could fly down to Key West from Connecticut with a girlfriend, and go sailing with me on my new boat. Sara was also interested in going sailing with a girlfriend and me. Four girls, a sailboat, a large bag of pot, and a somewhat-naive captain. How could that be a bad thing?

Connie and her friend called from Sloppy Joe's Bar and requested an immediate extraction. I rushed over to the bar and informed the sharks circling the two girls that it was time to board their yacht, and they had to go right now. Sloppy Joe's is not for amateurs. We fled to the marina and got comfortable for the night. Sara and her friend arrived early the next morning, and we cast off for the Dry Tortugas. The trip was seventy-eight miles to the west of Key West. We followed the island chain, as the girls got comfortable sunning topless on the forward deck. A coast guard cutter burned a lot of fuel getting close enough to investigate the foredeck. They turned off after they had confirmed that we were not smuggling Cubans, just naked women. Considering we were carrying a bag of pot on board, I was glad to see them turn away. We continued on to Loggerhead Key and anchored off the Coast Guard dock for the night.

Loggerhead Key is a one-mile-long crescent-shaped island with a lighthouse planted right in the middle. The US Coast Guard has the use of a beautiful old wooden two-story lightkeeper's house for sleeping and a separate cement block building used as a recreation room. It sports a pool table and a bar. Imagine, a federal agency actually encouraging drinking. It appeared that the isolation of this duty was compensated by a large and frequent supply of beer and pool chalk. There was a magnificent reef surrounding the island. White-sand beaches and a Boston Whaler equipped with a set of water skis were also supplied to keep the boredom away. The only thing that was missing was, of course, women. Imagine their glee when they looked out onto the anchorage and spotted a sailboat sporting four lovely mostly naked women sunbathing on the forward deck.

I slipped over the side early the next morning looking for breakfast and hoping for a big fish for a party on the beach later in the day. This was not my first time as a visitor to the Tortugas, but it had been at least five years. I'm sure there were regulations on spearfishing in the park, but ignorance of the law was my excuse. The water was not as clear as the Bahamas and Turks and Caicos, but no water is. I quickly speared two blue runners and stowed them in the dinghy. I had spent so much time in the water over the last few years it was like coming home. There were other carnivores—barracuda and grouper—also cruising for breakfast along with me. It is always a good idea to keep track of your competition, especially barracuda. When you do spear the right fish, it is best to get your prize out of the water quickly or at least leave the fish on the end of the spear rather than letting it slide down the shaft to your hand. Barracudas do not discriminate between hands and fish.

A huge hogfish was cruising in the turtle grass just below me. As I jackknifed in his direction, he sensed the danger and slowly turned to run. Grouper and hogfish both have a habit of turning broadside to check on the progress of any pursuer. At that moment, they displayed a large and transitory target. I was cocked and ready for this moment. The big fish turned, and I released the spear. This is a Zen moment, a mind-body dance where you become the spear. The fiberglass spear is propelled by a loop of surgical tubing attached to the north end of the spear. You slide the loop between your thumb and forefinger and slide your hand along the spear until it is stretched tight. You acquire the target and release your grip. The spear will stay in your hand, or at the very least, the rubber loop will stay clutched in your fingers. If you miss, the reload process is as quick as sliding your hand down the shaft again. I didn't miss. I shoved the spear through the fish and into the bottom to prevent escape. Out of air, I headed for the surface hauling the spear and the fish behind me. We were now ready for scrambled eggs and blue runners, fried in olive oil with sweet onions. The hogfish was for dinner.

We spent the day snorkeling on the magnificent crown reef festooned with elkhorn coral and giant five-hundred-pound grouper. The giant grouper in South Florida have succumbed to hook-and-line fishing and speargun fishing with explosive power heads. The elkhorn coral disappeared in the mid-1990s and is slowly coming back after a worldwide loss. We were lucky to see these beautiful sights. Hopefully, they will return.

Late in the afternoon, after gutting and cleaning the hogfish, I grabbed some aluminum foil, scooped up some chopped vegetables, and rowed over to the beach. It was easy to dig a pit in the soft coral sand. I gathered some driftwood and placed it into a cavity in the sand and set it on fire. The hard tropical woods burned down into hot coals perfect for cooking the big fish stuffed with onions, potatoes, and carrots. I covered the fish and fire with some damp Sargassum weed to create a little steam and hold in the heat. It was time for a cold beer.

Just as I started my beer, I was politely interrupted by a young coastie.

"Sir, you can't have a fire on the beach, it's a national park, you know."

"Well, the fish will be done pretty soon. Why don't you get the rest of the guys and some coast guard beer? The girls will be over here as soon as the spaghetti and meatballs are done."

He immediately put all the possibilities together and forgot about the illegal fire and ran to encourage his mates to abandon their post and come and have dinner with the four girls. I rowed out to *Good Fortune* and loaded up the girls and the huge pot of pasta, with at least fifty meatballs. During a short tour of the island, the lightkeeper revealed to me that there was a single-sideband radio in the top of the lighthouse for monitoring drug traffic in the Caribbean. I thought that was a great idea, considering the location on the junction of the Gulf of Mexico and the Straits of Florida, and it gave the guys something to do other than fishing, swimming, and waterskiing.

All of us gathered around the fire, occasionally poking the fish to see if it was done. Connie passed the plate heaped with steaming meatballs and spaghetti. Ten people hit the pot with great enthusiasm and left the restaurant-sized cooking vessel empty in no time. I opened the aluminum foil to reveal a perfectly cooked hogfish, which went well with all the beer supplied by the Coast Guard crew. To make the whole affair almost perfect, a full moon erupted out of the ocean and beamed a river of golden light on our party. It seemed almost spiritual until it seemed too spiritual.

Connie was grinning like the Cheshire cat, and my suspicious gene was going off. I noticed that most of the crowd was lying on the sand, giggling and staring into the bowl of stars. Connie had laced the meatballs with pot. This would only be a problem if there was anyone not stoned in our group of ten. Since we were all practicing carnivores, we were all completely stoned for at least the immediate future. I can't be certain if any of my crew made it back to the boat that night, but I can be certain that any Caribbean drug traffic that occurred that night was not monitored by the personnel of the coast guard light station in Loggerhead Key.

The sun brought a semblance of mental order, enough to assemble the crew onto the boat and sail out into the Gulf of Mexico for most of the day until brain function was restored. We spent the rest of our time in the Tortugas enjoying nature and not eating any more meatballs. The Coast Guard never bothered us again, and the bag of pot was eventually smoked or given away to friends. My friend Sam, who finally took the pot from the trash can, managed to wash the salt water out of the ninety-five pounds. Unfortunately, the pillowcase the pot was in came untied and made a mess of the commercial washer in his trailer park laundromat. He had a lot of fun, I'm sure, telling this story to friends and relatives. Sam helped me out with a year's worth of boat payments eventually. Everyone was happy.

Another Jo

In between college groups, I realized that catering to tourists was a great filler. In the right weather conditions, my routine was to motor around to the ocean side of Key West, traverse a narrow channel, and anchor off the Casa Marina Hotel. The water off the pier was just deep enough to float the boat with four inches under the keel. People would come down and hang around to look at the beautiful water and *Good Fortune* sitting at anchor. I would row over in the skiff and hang out on the pier to talk with people and encourage them to go sailing with me. One day, I noticed an olive-skinned guy leaning on the rail. This was not the first time I had seen him, so I struck up a conversation.

"You must be on vacation."

"No, I live here, my girlfriend works here at the hotel."

"I've seen you here on the dock, what do you do?"

"I'm a treasure hunter."

That was code for "I'm a drug smuggler." So I decided to poke the bear and see what happened.

"How's that working for ya?" I exclaimed.

"The damn DEA took my boat on a trumped-up charge." The bear snapped back. "They planted a bale of pot in the mangroves where I was working and roared up in their boat and accused me of smuggling. Just because I was near it, they accused me of owning it and took my boat. What do you think of that?"

Talk about a loaded question. Backpedaling, I let him know that I had no use for the DEA. He then went on ranting at length about how they pestered him all the time and just would not let him treasure hunt and make an honest living. I established an emotional distance and assured him that since he was obviously innocent, things would get better.

This whole conversation was a charade to feel me out on the subject of smuggling and assorted adventure jobs. He then invited me to dinner with his girlfriend. This was a get-to-know-Ron party for "Jo" and his employer, Juan, up in Miami. Jo was not a threat, just a microphone that I spoke into, and the bosses in Dade Co. listened. I figured they would shadow me just to confirm my stories, and Jo was the shadow. So far I had met Miami Juan and Jo with no last names. I did have phone numbers for both, but I never called either one.

Hugo's Back

On the fifteenth of February, Hugo called. He said, "I'm in Fort Lauderdale. I'm on my new boat, my father's here, my girlfriend is here, my father's girlfriend is here. We are having a party, and I have your papers. Come on up."

I fired up the Toyota and headed for Broward County. *Remember* was the first boat name I saw when I pulled into the Riverbend boat-yard. The name was gold-leafed on the stern of a nine-foot draft, sixty-seven-foot fiberglass yacht, towering over the rest of the boats in the yard. The stairway up to the deck was two stories high with safety rails. This was a big boat. *Don Bosco* was also out of the water and also quite large in comparison to the rest of the yachts. I scaled the stairs, reached the deck, and searched out the main hatch. I could smell fine cuisine wafting from the interior of the boat. A shaft of light indicated the entrance and the ladder down below. I hailed Hugo, and he immediately appeared in the glow of the interior light.

"Come down below, Ron, we have been waiting for you."

"Thanks, I have been waiting for you." We both laughed and did a manly embrace, not too tight. A young woman slipped by holding a plate of food fully engulfed in flames.

"Dinner is ready, you are just in time," Hugo announced.

The cabin was very large with a settee for eight on one side of the cabin. An elderly man in a blue jumpsuit and two lovely women were situating themselves around a lot of flaming food. Huge glasses of red wine seemed dangerously close to the open flame of the still-burning food. Hugo motioned me into a spot, and I immediately extinguished my meal with a big puff. Everyone laughed, and Hugo told me the alcohol would have burned off soon without having to blow it out. This crowd was seriously drunk, and my arrival may have saved them all from burning alive in a fiberglass tomb. I mentioned that to them, and they all laughed uncontrollably when translated into French for the cook.

We had a grand meal, and even some of the drinks were served on fire. Hugo showed me around his new boat. The vessel had seven double-sleeping cabins, three heads, forward crew quarters, and a master stateroom with a queen-size bed and a built-in piano. All the upholstery was glove leather, and linen curtains hung from all the ports. *Opulent* was the word.

A stack of paperwork greeted me at the breakfast table in the morning. Most of it was in French and some in German. None of it was in English. Hugo explained that the boat had been chartered once in the South of France and washed up on a beach on its beam. There was a lot of cosmetic damage to the gel coat, and the rudder was damaged. I recognized the repair-work documents and insurance-company paperwork. The original builder's certificate from Tyler Molding in England and the paperwork from Anne Wever in Holland were also there. That was enough for me, so I told Hugo we just needed to work up a bill of sale with a payment schedule. We worked out the financials and then discussed my staying in Fort Lauderdale to broker *Don Bosco*. At $185,000, *Don Bosco* seemed like a deal. I would have taken 10 percent of the sale price for a broker fee, which would have squared me with Hugo. I really did not want to stay in the city and deal with that big boat, so I begged off. There was still a chance I could bring the boat to Key West and live on it or use it for the college charters. *Don Bosco* had a draft, in the neighborhood, of eight feet, not a great Florida Keys boat where the average depth is five to six feet.

Life had just become a little less complicated, at least in Hugo's camp. Our dealings, aside from the financials, were over with, I thought. We all finally collapsed into any bunk close by and slept well into the next day.

THE BEAT GOES ON

I left Hugo and his crew in Fort Lauderdale and went back to Key West. I had booked an expedition-type charter in the Bahamas for late March. There were lots of things to do to get ready. It was three hundred miles from Key West to Nassau in the Gulf Stream and across the shallow Bahama Banks. A young fellow from Scotland had sailed in from the Bahamas on a private boat several weeks before and was partied out and ready to return home to the Bahamas. His family had immigrated to the Bahamas, so he was in line for citizenship. I agreed to take him on as crew for both his advantage and mine. We left Key West early in hopes of beating the increasing easterly winds later in the day.

No such luck; the waves were six footers on the bow for ten hours just to get to Marathon, fifty miles away. We went ashore, had Mexican food, and turned in for another early start.

First light guided us out of the harbor and into the Hawk Channel. The wind had backed to the northeast, so we could hoist the number 2 jib and sail out into the Gulf Stream. We crossed the barrier reef and out into deep water. The Stream was running northeast at about three knots, and the wind was blowing from the northeast at thirty knots. This made for a very short horrible sea smashing against the port bow. A wave crossed over the bow and into the jib, tearing it to pieces. I quickly started forward to pull the jib down when I bumped into a rigging wire hanging loose from the mast. The impact from the wave had demolished the cast-lock fitting that secured the aft lower shroud. I pulled down the jib, rolled it up, stuffed it in a bag, and dragged it back to the cockpit. My crew had held the course, so we were making good time without the jib. I jumped down below and dove into the gear locker again to find the wire clamps. They had rusted again, so it took a little time to free them up enough to reuse them. After this trip, I purchased several different-size clamps in stainless to avoid the ever-present rust problem. Within a few years, I changed every fitting on the boat, including the ones in the locker, to stainless.

I sat on the cabin top and fashioned a loop into the broken wire, attached a rusty shackle, with a piece of chain hanging from it, to the loop and then down to the turnbuckle. Once it was adjusted, all was well, and it was time to hoist the storm jib. As we trimmed the jib, the boat surged forward, and we were on our way. We careened through the waves all night at speeds exceeding twelve knots. We were going so fast we overshot Gun Cay in the dark, and by the time the sun came up, we were motoring due south against the current to get back to Gun Cay.

As we sailed into the harbor, the first boat I saw was *Don Bosco* anchored to the wind. It had been a year since I had seen her, and I was eager to see who was on board. There was no one on board as I rowed close abeam and hailed. As I looked toward the shore, I noticed an individual watching me. The Boston Whaler skiff was a great rowboat, and I gained the shore in a few minutes. The stranger greeted me and asked if I knew him.

"No, actually I do know your boat and its former owner."

"It certainly is a small boating world." He helped me pull the skiff up on the beach and began to pump me for information.

"Do you know where Hugo is?

"The last I knew, he was sailing around the world in his new boat, why?" I asked.

"Well, he took my money and left me with a substantial yard bill on the boat."

"How much was the bill, if you don't mind saying."

"It was $165,000."

He flinched when I slapped him on the back and invited him to join the club. He smiled philosophically and remarked that he, deep down, was an optimist, but his faith in Hugo was waning. I passed him my newly minted business card and asked him to let me know how his story ends. No word yet. With the help of the Internet, I now know that *Don Bosco* has found a home in Costa Rica as a charter boat. She seems to be doing well and will probably live a long time with good owners.

AND YOU ARE WHO?

Hugo was gone. The wake left by three years of drug-smuggler high jinks in the Caribbean and South Florida rippled into every corner of my usual haunts. It seemed like every place I traveled with *Good Fortune*, I would run into former *Fortunella* alumni.

After years of group chartering, I had burned out as the sole operator of the galley, boat and the engine room. I had a small altercation in a bar in Key West, which left me persona non grata on the waterfront. My friend Howard was sitting in Miami with his Durbeck 46, ready to do some chartering. His boat-building project had started with a younger girlfriend, about ten years earlier, and a dream to charter in the warm tropical waters of the Bahamas. The girlfriend met a younger sperm donor and departed midboat project. In a post-girlfriend-departure funk, Howard backslid on construction to the point where the decline in the state of the boat's health exceeded progress in construction. I suggested I might be able to use his boat in conjunction with mine to carry and instruct students in my new charter venture. The thought of young female college students on board his new boat gave Howard just the kick he needed to push for the finish line. Now that I had parked *Good Fortune* in a boatyard in Stock Island, I bussed to Miami to meet him and *Heart's Desire* at Dinner Key Marina.

We welcomed aboard a larger-than-planned group, self-named the Duke Sailing Club. Federal law limits the passenger count to six on charter yachts under one hundred tons. The Duke group numbered eleven. We were leaving the country and sailing to a foreign country that had no passenger limits. We did not have eleven bunks down below, but since they were there, we had no choice but to take them and hope we would not be boarded before we gained the high seas. The students brought fifty cases of beer with them, so we loaded them and their beer onto the boat. Howard renamed them the Duke Drinking Club.

We tossed the lines from Dinner Key Marina and had a very pleasant crossing of Biscayne Bay and the Hawk Channel. When we crossed the barrier reef, *Hearts Desire* immediately plunged into a violent sea fueled by the southeast trade winds and tortured by the Gulf Stream. The port rail of *Heart's Desire* scooped up every passing wave while the windward bow offered a sheer wall for breaking seas, whose spume cascaded over the entire boat and joined the stream of water on the lower rail. A group of students scrambled down the companionway steps to the cavernous main cabin and began to drink beer and eat chips. The drinkers emerged, white-faced and clammy, to seek the port rail and that constant stream of refreshing Gulf Stream water. One coed lashed herself to the deck looking like a crucified prophet, while others tucked into a fetal position in the deck wash. Used beer and chips mingled with the sea.

Our arrival at Gun Cay in the Bahamas was a welcome relief from seasickness, and the rest of the crowd was eager to really start drinking. The plan was to let everyone enjoy the beautiful water and sunshine while slurping down large amounts of beer and weigh anchor in the evening to sail across the Bahama Banks at night.

Howard and I rose early to prepare a hearty breakfast for the hungover crew. We were aware that another group of Duke students had hired another boat to meet us in the anchorage behind Gun Cay. While I was sitting in the cockpit, sipping a hot cup of coffee, I noticed a spiral of smoke rising from the cabin top of a Morgan Out Island moored right next to us. I immediately jumped into the dinghy and rowed as hard as I could toward the burning boat. Peering over my shoulder, I saw a young man outside on the deck waving at me. There was a five-gallon bucket in the rowboat. I grabbed it and filled it with water as soon as I reached the boat and handed it to the student. He doused the fire several times as I refilled the bucket each time. By now everyone on board was on the deck. The smoke was still inside the boat and also venting through the hole in the cabin top.

This same scenario had occurred on *Good Fortune* just a few months earlier, causing the kerosene stove to explode, blowing quiche and soot all over the main cabin. A quick cleanup was all it took to repair the damage. The Morgan actually caught on fire and now had a hole in the cabin top. This damage renders the boat unseaworthy and unusable with paying passengers on board.

I offered my condolences and queried them about their plans after the fire. They told me that they were the other Duke group and would I let them continue with me on *Heart's Desire*. I laughed and informed them that the best thing for them was to travel a short distance to Bimini Island and book a passage back to Miami after they enjoyed Bimini and its beaches for a while.

The weather had plans of its own, so we set sail midafternoon for a long trip across the Bahama Banks. By midnight, I was left with one sober student and a whole lot of wind. The weather had deteriorated, and everyone had gone below, leaving me and a really tall student to struggle to take the mainsail down and then struggle to hoist the mizzen. During that struggle, my taller-than-average deckhand managed to wade through several of the food coolers tied to the back deck. Driving around a pair of size-14 feet in pitching seas, while trying to handle a large sail on the back deck, had released dozens of hard frozen steaks and pork chops Howard had purchased in Miami. Most of them washed over the side in the maelstrom and onto the menu of a passing carnivore.

Howard, being notoriously stingy, had purchased a less-expensive loran (long-range navigational aid) for this voyage. Since we were more than one hundred miles offshore, the unit was at its limit of functionality. With no functioning navigational gear on board, we were *dead reckoning* our way across the bank. The tidal currents are strong and unpredictable on the Bahama Banks, so I eventually just took down the sails and anchored until dawn. The morning revealed a Bahamian freight boat steaming toward us.

As they came abeam, a fella yelled, "Where we reach?"

We had a gam—that is, a discussion across the water between two boats, with the black fellas, and reckoned our position to the satisfaction of all. We set off to the east and them to the west. The chart indicated sand ridges (bars) running north-south, so we followed the ridges back down onto the bank again. We arrived in Chub Cay midday and tied up to another big sailboat full of spring breakers. Everything was well with the crew, but the transmission was slam full of seawater. The water-transmission-fluid mixture looked like mud and had to be removed and flushed with new transmission fluid. We moved a few cooling lines around and plugged up the old damaged portion of the cooler with some pipe plugs, and off we went. The transmission worked again, but the extra water inside the housing had forced the front seal to blow out and allowed transmission fluid to leak into the bell housing on the back of the engine. Howard and I decided to pull the plug from the bottom of the bell housing so the transmission fluid would drain into a milk jug placed under the engine.

Howard used an electric drill pump, with a zip tie on the trigger, to pump the fluid back into the transmission as fast as it leaked out. It worked perfectly, as long as there was someone in the engine room to monitor this arrangement. A button on a small electric box had to be pushed at the moment the engine reached 1,650 rpm. That would turn an alternator on, providing power at sixty cycles per second and 120 volts AC. Meanwhile, the drill pump was actuated, and the transmission was placed in gear. This operation took three people initially, and then a standing watch, to assure it all continued as planned. Howard and I praised all involved and confirmed that they were eager learners and worthy of their parents' tuition money.

Off we went, across the Tongue of the Ocean, to Nassau, Howard and me and eleven college students on *Heart's Desire*. The sunset was over our stern as we made our way into Nassau Harbour. We were too late to get a slip for the evening, so we anchored off the dock in a small basin with several Bahamian fishing vessels. The bottom was solid limestone with a thin veneer of sand. Our big Danforth anchor settled onto the bottom. We tugged on it by hand, and it seemed secure. Fatigue is the father of disaster. It was calm in the basin, so why spend a lot of time messin' with the anchor? There were so many wrecks on the bottom it was bound to hook on something.

We all turned in early since most of the beer had chafed through the thin cheap aluminum cans and fizzled into the bilge without passing through a college student's digestive system. For the last part of the voyage, the bilge pump had been the kidney of the boat, digesting and spewing flat cheap beer into the ocean.

I slept on the cockpit seat on this part of the trip. I was zipped up in my sleeping bag when I heard a large thump on the stern of the boat. The first sight to greet me, as I poked my head out of the bag, was the side of a very large boat. My limbic system kicked into overdrive when I realized we were lying on the side of a ship tied to the commercial pier.

"All hands on deck," I screamed, and two kids erupted from the hatch.

I started the engine while one of the kids excited the alternator and another plugged in the drill pump. Howard took the helm, and three of us ran forward to retrieve the anchor. When it broke the surface, it had a conch shell installed on each fluke, most assuredly by Puck, the mischievous spirit from *A Midsummer Night's Dream*. I noticed that the fuel dock was open and motioned to Howard to bring her around. He laid her on the dock just as the wind surged to sixty knots or thereabouts. We all jumped onto the dock and pushed on the gunnels of *Heart's Desire* in a vain attempt to ameliorate damage to the hull. Soaked to the skin and cold, we climbed aboard as the wind abated. We dodged a major bullet when we dragged into the freighter. Our conch-laden anchor would not have kept us from dragging into the marina and causing a lot of damage to other yachts and docks. Thanks, Puck.

The Duke Drinking Club was scheduled to depart the boat in Nassau, and Howard and I had our work cut out for us repairing the transmission. This large chunk of cast iron needed to be removed from the engine and the front seal on the spline shaft replaced. This little seal was less than $5 in Miami and easy to find. This was not Miami, so the cost would be much higher—if we could even find one. We did a radio survey of the local boats and found a cruiser that had located a shop in town with the seals we needed, hanging on the shop wall. I rented a motor scooter and headed for the shop. When I arrived, a cordial old fellow was glad to sell me a handful of seals for the Miami price. He told me he brings them in by the case because there is such a demand. That was the easy part.

We spent the next two days yanking that damn tranny off the back of that engine and scooting it along the floor to the main cabin. The seal replacement was very simple; the reinstallation on the engine was torture.

Our next group of passengers was two couples from Georgia that worked for the Department of Agriculture. They made their daily bread sitting at a desk receiving mail, reading it, and filing it. Decisions were about the school lunch program and what to do on their next vacation; Howard and I were their decision.

They arrived with hard square wheeled luggage, great for navigating an airport but not so great for a boat. We knew we were in trouble when we saw the luggage. In the old days, 1984—and we were still in the old days—a pantry on a boat had square sides and a square fiddle in the front to hold the contents of the pantry. The dishes were square and made of wood, unbreakable, with a raised edge. Food would stay on the plate long enough to eat it, and the plate would nest in the cabinet nicely with no waste of space. This was the origin of the phrase "square meal." The rest of the boat was much happier with luggage that squished and bent to conform to the curve of the hull or the side of the bunk and its occupant. Sailors live this way; lubbers rarely do.

The charters settled in with a little room to spare for the luggage, and we cleared the dock for the anchorage. The weather was not settled, so we decided to anchor out and bring the skiff ashore for last-minute ice-and-alcohol shopping. All six of us piled into the twelve-foot skiff and headed to the closest dock near the rum store. I noticed a fiberglass express cruiser heading for the fuel dock with two inappropriately dressed guys on the foredeck. Muscle T-shirts, black tight long pants, and shit-kicking pointed shoes stood out as nonnautical accoutrements in the world of boating folks. These guys looked familiar to me. As we closed on the cruiser, I realized I had seen the two guys in Provo and Miami.

The world shrunk to neighborhood size as I tried to not look like myself. With a huge mop of blond hair and a bigger beard, I felt like a sore thumb in the bright sun. I grabbed Howard's hat and stuffed it on my head, leaving Howard's bald head gleaming in the sun.

"Wise guys," I said to Howard.

He shrugged and goosed the throttle. We sped by, and I finally exhaled; these guys were definitely Roy Pigeon and another unnamed smuggler from Miami. I guess to them, I was just another Anglo on a boating holiday. As we passed under their bow and down their side, I quipped loud enough so they could hear, "They need to hire some Anglos."

Yes, I know that was stupid, but sometimes I just have to poke the bear. They heard me but probably had no chance to identify the culprit as we sped away. Our visit to the rum store was a complicated process of trying to decide what country and age and level of spice our rum would be. Everyone selected a different kind, and we all assembled at the dinghy dock for the trip back. Our little boat, with six adults stuffed into it, emerged from between the piers right next to the fuel dock. Sandwiched between a Bahamian defense force torpedo gunboat and the dock was the express cruiser from Miami. The crew stood facing the Esso sign with their hands above their heads. All the young Bahamian recruits had guns drawn, so it looked like the gig was up. I mentioned to our passengers that they should have taken my advice and "hired some Anglos." Here's hoping they did not collect $200 but went directly to jail. We had a great laugh about the whole affair when we got back to the boat and confirmed that the sun was definitely over the yardarm.

I had never wanted to see these guys again, and there they were, on another smuggling/yachting holiday. Were they on a stolen boat? Did they have drugs aboard? Did they get caught? Who knows? I hope they stay clear of my course and leave me alone 'cause I'm just a live-and-let-live kinda guy.

We spent the next week cruising in the northern Exumas, visiting Allen and Highbourne Cays. The weather was cool and windy with more clouds than usual. While we were anchored one night, we heard a burst of radio traffic while we sipped rum and Cokes. We could hear helicopters south of us and cruising sailors remarking that it sounded like a war zone at Norman's Cay. I knew that the island was infested with dopers of the Colombian persuasion. Danny and I had anchored in the harbor on our northbound journey with *Fortunella* and had been asked to leave at the point of a very large automatic weapon on the back of a Jeep. We left. Now it sounded like a drug war or maybe some government stepping in to clean up the island.

We waited until the next day and contacted sailors that were located closer to the action. They let us know, to their best knowledge, that the druggies had been run off the cay, and it appeared that the troops were gone, and the looting had begun. Looting piqued Howard's interest, and he quickly suggested to our guests that we might include looting an abandoned drug island as a featured activity for our day's adventure.

We weighed anchor and headed south with great anticipation. As we came into the harbor at Norman's Cay, we saw several yachts were already anchored, and the Bahamian police were busily hauling tires to their police boat. It looked like everyone was enjoying the day with a little looting fever. We anchored and quickly reached the dock in our small skiff. Our first greeting was the Bahamian policeman with a delightful "Good day, mon," and off he went. We took that to mean "join in the looting." We spread out and began pilfering, at will, in the restaurant, the maintenance sheds, and the homes along the waterfront. It was like shopping after aliens abducted the entire population with no warning. The food in the restaurant was still on the plates, uneaten. The lights, radios, and air conditioners were all left running until the fuel ran out. Our scavenging was for souvenirs and some needed galley supplies. Okay, I did get a windsurfer, a set of fine English stoneware, a motorcycle, and a small refrigerator. This stuff was all purchased with drug money, dirty drug money.

The backstory was that the US military contacted the Bahamian government and asked/told Pindling, the prime minister, that they would really like to send a black ops crowd onto Norman's Cay and kick some Colombian butt. It was well known that the Colombians were the paid guests of the Pindling government, so why would the prime minister not call and let his guest know about the impending invasion? He did, and they scurried away in their airplanes and left nothing but an island behind. How disappointing for the black ops people. The Colombians never returned, so I guess it worked.

We had a great sail back to Nassau, which helped wash the disappointing weather out of our guests' memory. The pillaging was also a break from their bureaucratic life back in the States. By the time we arrived in Nassau, the crew was ready to see the town and do a little gambling. When they were departing the next day, they paid for the entire trip in local currency, which they had won at the blackjack table the night before. Of course we were glad to get paid, but it did hurt to know that our guest had simply won the money in a card game. Howard and I considered taking up the game of 21 and getting out of the charter business.

Our next charter was my group of six students and John Iverson from Earlham College in Indiana. This is the same college that had attended my tropical biology course back in Pine Cay. I had lost track of John, the professor, for a while but had rediscovered him on the front cover of *Outward Bound* magazine. A customer in Key West had brought the magazine to me because he thought I might be interested in working with *Outward Bound*. A quick glance at the inside flap, and I realized that this was Dr. John. He was a former graduate student on Pine Cay, working with the indigenous iguanas. He had provided Chuck and me with our first in situ educational group after he secured his PhD and an inland job far from his study animals. Science jobs were not easy to come by. John ended up in Indiana at a small four-year Quaker college that had sprouted out of the left paw of that pacifist religious group. I immediately contacted Dr. John and informed him of my new path on the educational frontier. He was excited to learn about the boat and was eager to join me in the Bahamas on his study island. The trip from Miami to Nassau proved long and harrowing for a Duke group I had contracted to for the sail to Nassau.

I had already taken the Earlham group to the Exumas once from the port of Nassau and was very glad to just have thirty-five miles of relatively protected water to bring this group to Allen's Cay.

Howard and I were scheduled to pick up Dr. John's group of students and deliver them to Allen's Cay, a short thirty-five-mile hop across the Yellow Bank. We left Nassau Yacht Haven as soon as breakfast was over and headed east out of the harbor. I instructed all the students, no matter what flavor their skin color was, to apply copious amounts of lotion with sunscreen. This was not my first rodeo with white pasty Midwestern students. They burn faster than a flour tortilla in a hot skillet. The rest of the trip would be miserable with a bout of sun poisoning. By the time they arrived in Nassau, from the middle of the continent, they were ready to get a little shut-eye; if they did get seasick—and they did—they were already in their bunks. Nobody but Howard and I were hungry at lunchtime, so I bagged up all the lunch and waited until we reached our destination. On cue, everyone was ready to eat as soon as we dropped anchor.

While the students sat eating their lunch, twenty or so iguanas would gather on the small beach just off our beam. The animals know our arrival, or any other boats' arrival, will bring much-appreciated food in their direction.

We instructed the students about this behavior and how they could use food in the hand to bring them in close enough to catch by hand or net. Yes, we were on a sanctioned lizard hunt. What could be better?

When our twelve-foot skiff hit the beach, the students tumbled out into the gin-clear azure water, trying not to go swimming before they go hunting. If they swam first, their sun protection would wash off and require reapplication. Our time was limited on the island, and we needed to get the work done and then go swimming at the end of the first day. I instructed them that it was best to approach the animals slowly and deceitfully, not letting on that the net in your hand was intended for capture. Once the iguana was in the net, the student must carefully grasp the animal by the back of the neck and slide it into a waiting pillowcase, held by another student. It did not take long before our pasty Midwesterners were bagging iguanas as fast as they could catch them. Meanwhile the adults were setting up a shade shelter and chairs so that the process of measuring, weighing, and sexing our captors can go on smoothly in relative comfort out of the tropical sun. All the above-mentioned iguana activity is accompanied by a fifteen-knot-plus wind, which is great for cooling the hunters but does hamper almost all other activities. As a sailor, I always cling to the adage that the wind is your friend. If you are not paying attention, it can get less friendly.

We spent two days catching iguanas on Leaf Cay and then moved the boat about four hundred yards to U-Cay and set up our shade shelter and tagging team. When I dropped off the first group of students, I noticed two Bahamian fishermen on the beach sitting on an outboard motor. There were the broken remains of a fiberglass boat in the corner of the U-shaped beach, which I assumed was the remains of their boat. They told me that they had been shipwrecked for three days. They asked if we could spare some food and water until their friends came to get them. We helped them out, and in return, they gave Howard a very large anchor that was on their boat but not in use during the storm. The boat evidently went ashore so fast they had no time to use it. The wind was not their friend, and they were not paying attention. This was a strong lesson for them and me. Always pay attention. To this day, thirty years later, the remains of that wreck still show at low tide, and now I am the proud owner of that seventy-five-pound Luke anchor. Learning a lesson the hard way is always the best way. Pain is mental cement.

The last charter of our winter season was our return to Miami with a group of elementary-school teachers from a small town in the Central Appalachians. I say this so you may formalize a mental picture of the conservative culture and politics of the region where these folks lived and worked. Everyone was new to the tropics, and each had a mental image about what this trip would be like on their vacation journey to Miami. When you sail west, at the latitude of the Central Bahamas, the wind is almost always at your back. That means you have achieved nirvana for sailing. "May the wind be at your back" is as good as it gets.

The thirty-five-mile journey across the Tongue of the Ocean was smooth and sunny. We sailed into Frazer's Hog Cay and dropped anchor. The trip had acclimated all to the rigors and rewards of ocean sailing. Everyone was sitting in the cockpit of *Heart's Desire* looking at the palm-fringed shore and crystal-clear water, contemplating a swim, with or without swimsuits, when Howard vaulted from the hatch into the sea without a suit. The decision had been made. Within minutes, all were swimming with Howard, *without*. The rest of the trip to Miami was smooth and sunny, and all were *without*. Changes in latitude and changes in attitude, that's what vacation is all about. Thanks, Jimmie.

We secured *Heart's Desire* and said goodbye to our newly tanned teachers but not before some of them posed topless next to a carved topless figurehead on the bow of a big ketch moored next to us. That was the cherry on the cake for old Howard. He was eternally indebted to me for that charter and later sold his half of a small marina in Morehead City, North Carolina, to me at a very reasonable price. Thank you, Howard. I bet those teachers didn't show their students those pictures.

I needed to get back to Stock Island and *Good Fortune*. I took a couple of local Miami buses to get to the Greyhound station. When I boarded, I couldn't help but notice a guy walking in front of me with a ball cap, red backpack, and a fishing pole looking for a seat. He was Japanese for sure. The name Turiyaki was sewn on his cap, along with Disney World. I speak a little Japanese, so I sat next to him and introduced myself. He was elated to find a companion on the bus ride to the Keys. This guy was the epitome of a Japanese tourist. Our first stop was for lunch at the Burger King in Islamorada. The new restaurant had a sportfishing boat flybridge right in the middle of the seating area. Turiyaki and I sat at the helm seat. By now I had related the fact that I had a boat waiting for me in Key West. I thought it might be fun to ask him if he would like to sail to Miami with me. His tour group was somewhere in New England, and his only mission was to link up with them in New York in a couple of weeks. Fortunately, I had an English-Japanese dictionary on the boat; you never know when you will need one. I asked my new little mate if he would be interested in sailing with me to Miami. He jumped up and started to pantomime, swabbing the deck of our restaurant boat. Everyone in the bus group enjoyed his antics. An elderly woman came over and asked what had happened, so I told her I was going to take my new friend on a sailboat trip. She immediately asked if she could go also. I told her it would be a long torturous journey with sea serpents and towering freak waves. She shied away and told me she was looking for more of a luxury tour.

When we pulled abeam of Stock Island, I jerked the stop chord, and Turiyaki and I stepped off the bus and walked a mile to the boat-yard. He was stunned by the size of the boat and his great good luck. We went to a Japanese restaurant for dinner and then to the Winn Dixie to stock up. I just let him point at stuff, and then I would put it in the cart. Nothing makes a boat trip like great food. We filled the cart with a bizarre array of international foods, including a case of Asahi beer. We were ready to go. The bottom of the boat was ready to paint, so we set to painting first thing in the morning. With two guys pushing the paint rollers, the job went quickly. The plan was to let the paint dry while we drove into Key West to see the sights. I was bent over cleaning the roller when a white Cadillac convertible screeched to a stop right in front of the *Good Fortune*. The driver got out of the car and stood for a moment, just looking at the boat and me. He was dressed in a bright-orange jumpsuit. Not the kind you get in prison, the kind your wear if you are from the Caribbean, like Jamaica.

"What jew doin' wit' dis boat, mon?" Erupted from his mouth.

"I'm paintin' the bottom. What's it to ya?"

"Dis boat woirks outa Miami, and I dun some crewin' on 'er. You got some need for crew?"

"I own this boat, and she's out of that business now."

"What kinda business you in now, mon?"

"Just chartering some now."

"You make good money doing dat? You sure you don't need crew?"

"No, I'm legal and happy. In fact, that little fella over there is my new and only crew."

Turiyaki and the jumpsuit guy locked eyes for a moment.

"When you leavin' this yard?"

"We will be here for a couple of days. I still need to fix some things.

"Good."

By the time we concluded our conversation, Jumpsuit had worked his way right into my personal space. He was hovering right off my bow, so to speak, and my fight genes were rallying the troops. He was a foot taller than me, so my only plan was a swift Irish kick in the nuts. Pirate stands aside. I think he considered me a potential new boss and decided to step back.

Jumpsuit walked quickly back to his massive automobile, got in, and slammed the door. He left a rooster tail of rocks as he fishtailed out of the boa yard.

Turiyaki had stepped behind the rudder to shield himself from the flying rocks. When he peeled out, I shouted to him, in my best Japanese, to finish the painting very quickly because we were leaving soon. Bob, the yard owner, saw this interaction from his office porch and was now coming down from the landing to get clued in. I decided to hold the clews and ask for an immediate launch, like right now. Bob headed for the travel lift and scaled the ladder to the driver's seat. Bob's secretary gave me a number to write on the check over the loudspeaker; I wrote the check and handed it to Bob as he glided the travel lift around the boat. We stood back and watched *Good Fortune* lift off the jack stands, rise up, turn and head for the launch bay. I could see the questions and excitement in Turiyaki's eyes, but I lacked the linguistic skills to explain thoroughly how bad it would be if Mr. Jumpsuit returned, and we were still there. As far as I knew, there was still a scheduled hit on the guy who took *Fortunella* from the stealers. We were certainly not going to stay around and see who might be invited to that party.

Getting on board a newly painted boat is always exciting. The boat will never be faster and slipperier than the day it is launched with a new paint job on the bottom. This may have been the first time my young friend had ever been on a boat. We jumped from the side of the lift bay onto the deck, reattached the head stay, and set up the turnbuckle. The seawater refilled the cooling system and the marine heads as we motored out the long channel to the coral lagoon that formed the protected waters inside the barrier reef.

A ninety-degree turn to port brought us on to a due-east heading as we passed the last channel marker. The coast is east-west in the Lower Keys directly into the northern edge of the trade winds. If the southeast winds were blowin', we would be in for some trouble, but fortunately, a front was on the way, bringing the wind to the southwest off our stern quarter. I rounded up to raise the main, then fell off and released the reefing line on the jib and the mule. Off we went. Turiyaki's eyes were opened wide as the long swell from the Florida Straits and a full set of sails pulled and pushed the big boat away from Key West and Mr. Orange Jumpsuit. Our destination was Marathon, fifty nautical miles due east.

The plan was to sail into the harbor at Boot Key and survey the marina with binoculars, hoping not to see Mr. Jumpsuit. We should be able to see him if he had the same clothes and the same "yank tank." It would not be good to be caught by a not-so-wise guy at this stage of the game.

A close friend of mine had her live-aboard boat repossessed while she was working and came home to an empty slip. She called me and asked what we could do about getting her boat back before the bank got their hands on it. Marathon was the next port the repo guys would put into, and if I knew seagoing repo guys, they would head for the bar as soon as the boat hit the dock. I suggested we could drive up the Keys and stake out the marina and steal the boat back while they were getting hammered at the tiki bar. Just as I guessed, they hurried up the dock as soon as the lines were secure to the dock cleats.

Kathy and I were milling around on the pier when they left the boat, and as soon as they disappeared into the bar, we jumped aboard, threw their gear on the dock, and used her spare key to start the engine and get underway. When we arrived in Marathon, Kathy had sent a blue-label express envelope with the money she owed the bank from the post office. The bank in Cincinnati would receive the money before we got back to Key West. The bank was cool about the whole thing; the contract repo guys were pissed off, and I'm sure they would have done something about it, so we put the boat in another marina on Stock Island for a couple of months, just in case.

This was all in the back of my mind as we slipped by Boot Key Marina, glassing the premises for Mr. Jumpsuit. Fortunately, he was not there, or in sight, but I still decided to anchor in the harbor as far from the landing as possible. We anchored in a tidal creek completely sheltered from any public view. You can never be too careful.

Turiyaki was chomping at the bit to learn how to row, so off we went, with my little Japanese-powered rowboat cutting a fine wake through the harbor. As I sat on the stern, watching Turiyaki flail at the water with the oars, I mused on the fact that we had actually defeated his nation of very enthusiastic people. Boy, were we lucky. I introduced Turiyaki to Mexican cuisine that evening, and while we were eating, he informed me that his profession back in Kyoto was cooking in a tempura restaurant. That explained his critique of my cooking at the end of each meal.

He would sit back, rub his belly, and exclaim, "Ah, typical American meal."

I handed him the keys to the galley for the duration of the trip and considered my job to be fish-catcher and beer-buyer.

Turiyaki and I arrived in Miami two days later and tied up next to Howard and *Heart's Desire*. I introduced my new friend to Howard and all his friends. When they found out that he was a professional cook, we all went to the Winn Dixie and bought whatever Turiyaki pointed at. The meal was on *Heart's Desire*, with half of the Dinner Key Marina in attendance. We ate and drank until Turiyaki had to go back to New York to catch his tour group. It was a sorrowful departure for all of us. I just wish he understood the meaning of being "greyhounded." That's what I told anybody that asked how I managed to get such a good cook on my boat. I would just tell them that I greyhounded him right off the bus. For those of you that do not understand, being shanghaied was the act of drugging sailors with alcohol or heroin and putting them aboard sailing ships bound for the Orient or other distant destinations. Living conditions on eighteenth-century sailing ships were not very good. The captains were taskmasters and considered the crew expendable compared to the ship's bottom line. They seldom got off the boat until the trip was over. Being greyhounded by Captain Ron was much better.

Howard and I stayed in Miami for a week to repair some of our seagoing damage and reunite with many of the friends we both knew in South Miami. Heading up the Gulf Stream with any wind out of the north was a very rough ride. It is much more pleasant to ride a south wind and the current when you head north. The other option is to motor sail up the Intracoastal Waterway. The first bridge on the waterway is the Julia Tuttle, arching across your path at a maximum height of fifty-five feet. The rest of the bridges, north to Norfolk, are sixty-five feet. The height restriction sends most ocean-going boats out the inlet into rather unpleasant conditions when wind and current are in opposition.

Howard left when the conditions were right and left me behind still doing repairs. I pulled away from the dock that afternoon and anchored in a small spot of deep water off a local watering hole. I decided to have a last supper and a beer in Coconut Grove for the year, so I rowed ashore and tied up to the seawall. The tide was low, making it difficult to scale the wall and the railing. It was Friday night, and the beer was cheap for a couple of hours. I ordered the grouper sandwich and a beer while I looked out at *Fortunella*, picturesquely anchored right in front of the bar window. The best grouper sandwich in South Florida was delivered to me next to a tall cold beer. I was just about to eat my sandwich when a female voice inquired.

"That boat out there is mine. Who are you?" I turned to confront a woman in a white nursing uniform.

"Get in line with half the people in Miami that think it's theirs," I said.

She was not amused. "My husband worked on that boat and is no longer alive."

"What's your name?"

"Debbie Rylie."

I immediately knew I was in trouble. When I first found the boat, John Rylie and Roy Pigeon were the two names on the Pan Am round-trip airline tickets in the drawer. After a year of looking at the tickets, every time I opened the chart table, I decided to go to the airport and see if I could cash them in. After some paperwork and subterfuge, Pan Am refunded the return fare on both tickets. Was Debbie Rylie the wife of John Rylie? Someone had told me that a crew member had been killed while on *Fortunella*.

All these questions were ruining in my mind as I stepped back, glanced at my beer, then at my sandwich, then at Debbie, and announced, "I have to hit the head." And I scurried into the men's room. As in most restaurants, the window in the head was narrow and lying on its side. My brain did a catlike calculation and determined that I could slither through, headfirst, and make a clean escape. I hated to leave the sandwich and beer behind, but I also needed to escape Miami and South Florida right then. The dumpster cushioned my fall as I nosed into a lot of cardboard and Styrofoam. Shaking parts of past meals off my tropical rock shirt, I headed around the corner of the building, slipped down the seawall, and into the skiff. Staying in the shadows, I rowed quickly out to the boat, scrambled forward, and commenced hauling the anchor in. With no lights or engine, I slowly drifted out into the bay as soon as the anchor came off the bottom.

When I felt I was clear of all danger, I started the engine and motored out the inlet and headed north in the Gulf Stream. The weather was unpleasant, and the seas were high and frequent. It was better than staying in Miami to see how many more former *Fortunella* alumni would show up and want to go down memory lane with her newest owner.

Debbie was the last person to make claim to the boat. As I have previously mentioned, I was told by the "businessmen" in Miami that an insurance company from Europe had made inquiries about the boat when they were operating it. I think they were just trying to frighten me away from the boat. It may be possible that Hugo was paid off by an insurance company and then paid by me also. If Hugo managed to double-sell his boat, it's on his karma, not mine.

I hoped to join Howard in North Carolina for a while and then head north for Newport, Rhode Island, to teach a marine science course for West Virginia Wesleyan. South Florida summers were long and hot, and Key West had proved too competitive and gnarly for me. My small charter business, with a maximum passenger limit of six people, had raised the dust on the charter dock in town. Entrenched local businesses were not happy to have my boat competing against them for the coveted tourist dollars. *Ecotourism*, as a word, had not been coined at that time. My fledgling underwater tour business was attracting attention from the other sail charter businesses. They were always wagging my brochure in my face and congratulating me on the best drug-smuggling cover ever. Their frustration with me, as an interloper, finally drove them to start pilfering my boat at every opportunity. No matter where the boat was tied up, it was a theft magnet. My insurance company wanted to get me off the books, so they canceled my insurance. My advertising brochures and posters were taken down and torn up as fast as I could put them out.

After a long day on the water, I decided to head for a local Key West watering hole for a beer-and-burger basket. The place was full of locals that spanned the gamut from boat crew to bon vivants.

I spotted a stool at the bar and started to sit down when a fellow brushed into me and jammed his finger into my ribs.

He leaned in and whispered, "If you don't leave Key West, you are going to get a shotgun up your scupper."

Now I was not in Vietnam or any battle that I know of in this lifetime, but I sure went into battle mode. I grabbed the guy by the crotch and the neck and launched him headfirst over the bar into the well drinks. The bartender skidded out of the way as he hit the floor drenched in booze. I leaned in over the bar and told him if I ever saw him again, I would kill him on sight. The island populace was so used to seeing this kind of behavior my actions were mostly ignored. I spun around and blew through the door, stopped for a moment to gather myself, and hopped onto my bike. Riding as hard as I could, I reached the marina in less than five minutes. It only took ten minutes for me to stow my motor scooter and bike on deck, start the engine, and cast off from the old concrete pier. I left the running lights off until I gained the ship channel and headed up to Stock Island to haul the boat out.

The next thing you know, I was standing in front of Debbie Rylie in a bar on the waterfront in Coconut Grove, brewing more fight-or-flight hormones for my next escape. A trip up the Gulf Stream away at sea and far from South Florida was the best plan for me.

Several days offshore put me abreast of the St. Johns River entrance in southern Georgia. Considering I had been sailing, cooking, fixing, and not sleeping well for two months, it was time to find a quiet anchorage and sleep safely for a while. I dropped anchor behind Cumberland Island and rested for a couple of days.

Offshore sailing is exhilarating, but it does wear you out, especially if you are alone. My plan was to slowly, eighty miles a day, work my way up the coast to someplace free of wise guys and other charter boats.

Georgia and South Carolina is a low meandering coast of spartina grass and deep tidal rivers. The going is slow, scenic, and demanding. Every turn of the channel is tracked on the chart and translated into action by me. At eight miles an hour, the day was slow and easy as long as I kept the boat in the channel. The best part of the day was finding a nice, quiet anchorage to drop the hook and cook a casual meal, usually on the grill. Three days of coasting brought me to an old spot just south of Southport, North Carolina. I passed a small narrow tidal creek with just enough room to swing on the hook at low water. I would have to spend some time getting the boat centered in the creek because the tidal range was six feet. Too close to the bank, and you wake up on your ear.

The boat was low on fuel, so I passed Dutchman's Creek and went on to stop at Southport Marina to get the tanks topped off. It had been a while since my last fill-up, so I put 170 gallons of diesel fuel in my twin tanks. Now I have to admit, the cosmetic appearance of my varnish was a little rough. Several years without electricity and hot water had left me with a pretty handsome beard and fairly long hair. There was still a portion of our society that labeled my appearance as a peace-loving hippie. Well, that was true. This hippie had a bank account and a credit card and a self-employed lifestyle. I offered the dockmaster a card, which matched the cards displayed on the window of the bait shop. He immediately informed me that it was cash in hand. I shrugged and headed for the New Testament for the needed cash. I opened the Good Book right on the chart table below the porthole. I did not realize that the person demanding the cash payment was standing in just the right position to see my not-so-secret hiding place. I passed him the correct change and asked for the water hose for a quick fill-up and a short deck rinse.

"Get your hippie ass out of here," was the response.

"I'm not going anywhere without that water hose," I responded tersely.

The radio sprung to life. "Southport Marina, this is the *Lady Weatherly* requesting fuel and dockage."

I knew this was an important call. Big boats take a lot of fuel and are charged a lot for overnight dockage. "Not leaving without water," was my refrain.

He threw the hose at me and yelled to be quick and get out.

Watered up and the deck cleaned of fuel, I gave a great push and cleared the dock so that the *Lady Weatherly* could take my place at the pier. Anchored securely in Dutchman's Creek for the night, I launched the Boston Whaler and headed into town for a nice Italian dinner and some grocery shopping. As I pulled heavily on the oars, two commercial fishing boats came out of the marina and roared by me and turned into the creek I had just come from. Nothing unusual. I reached the dock that I had been so rudely ejected from an hour earlier and tied to the back side, out of the way. The Piggly Wiggly was open and glad to see me. One grocery bag was all I could carry. The restaurant was next door, so I parked my bag next to a table and ate a good meal without having to clean up or cook.

Full inside and out, I headed back to the marina. As I passed the fuel shack, a dark figure stepped out of the shadows and grabbed me by the arm. My grocery bag tore open and spilled into the harbor. I realized there were two men close to me, so I sprinted back to the skiff and grabbed a seven-foot ash oar and then stood my ground. The older of the men approached me and verbally accused me of stealing a shower. I informed him that I had not one but two showers on my boat and that I had come ashore to buy groceries and have dinner. If I had come to take a shower, I would have asked and paid for it, and I would have a towel and soap with me.

I did offer to pay dockage for the ten-foot skiff for the hour that I had been there. He made an aggressive move toward me, and I jabbed him in the chest with the oar. The young man started down the dock, and I quickly informed him that it was none of his business and that I would make quick work of him with the oar. He turned and ran up the dock. I dropped the oar and invited the older man to step up and do his best. He turned and walked away.

That was too easy.

The floating portion of my groceries were within reach of the skiff, so I gathered them up and started rowing toward *Good Fortune*, as hard as I could pull. I coasted into the creek and scanned the dark shore, looking for the shadow of the masts in the backlit sky. Nothing, the boat was not where I left it. Rowing in circles, I crisscrossed the creek five or six times until I ran into a small yacht anchored in the upper reach of the creek. I hailed the owner and asked if they had seen my boat.

"Yes," they said. "It is on the other side of the waterway, lying completely over on her side."

My heart sank as I pulled heavily on the oars and crossed the channel to the dark shadow of the boat lying on the mud. There was no standing anywhere on the boat, so I wedged myself against the hull and fell asleep until dawn. The early light shed a depressing story of blatant theft and vandalism. The boat was no longer anchored, so I fished out a spare anchor from the locker and rowed it out into deep water and dropped it. The massive keel was resting lightly in the mud.

I had crawled out of the forward hatch at first light with just a T-shirt and started pumping the anchor winch handles. I was so used to being alone I did not worry about being mostly nude on the deck until I noticed the little Sam Croker-built Stone Horse sailboat quietly motoring by me. Bruce, the captain, hailed me and wished me good luck. All I could do was thank him and keep pumping on the winch handles. The anchor winch pulled the bow around into deep water. The engine finished the job. A survey in the morning light revealed the magnitude of the theft. It was clear now that the dockmaster was detaining me long enough for the two commercial boats to tie up to the boat and steal my marine radio, generator, cooler, main anchor right off the bottom, and all the money in the Good Book.

Without a radio, my only option was to get underway on the tide and head into town. Without life jackets, life ring, and flares, I would not pass an inspection by any state or federal water police. I needed to report the robbery to anyone who would listen and figure out what to do next. I tied up to two tired old pilings standing far enough away from the bank to make it necessary to dinghy ashore. I scrambled up the bank and stood upright in front of the local constabulary. He stretched out a hand and helped me up onto the top of the bank.

"Thanks, you folks need a town dock or something to welcome visitors."

He laughed and agreed with me. "People usually go the big state marina and walk into town."

"I tried that yesterday and received a less-than courteous welcome and was robbed last night by a couple of boaters from that marina."

"The guy that leases the marina from the state likes big expensive yachts that spend lots of money," said the cop.

"Well, as soon as I fill out a theft report with you folks and talk to the Coast Guard, I'm going to send a terse letter to the state attorney general and to the *Waterway Guide* about how I was treated at that marina."

The officer begged me to be kind to the local community and immediately blamed the theft on a "crabber from the county south of us." He offered to drive me around his county in search of my stolen gear. I showed him two polypropylene lines left tied to each side of the bow pulpit, cut with a sharp knife, and left behind.

"Two boats, huh."

"It looks that way."

"Let's see if we can find the boats that match those lines."

Riding shotgun, like Barney Fife and Andy, except this Andy was African American, we drove around the town and the county looking for the other end of those pieces of rope. We met a lot of nice people that were concerned and helpful but never found either boat or any of the gear. Everybody agreed that the marina had some issues, but no one was willing to indict the operator. The locals treated me well and passed on an old life jacket and some highway flares to help me get to a town with a marine supply store. I was left with twelve dollars and a checkbook from a Florida Keys bank. In those days, checks from a notorious string of islands populated by rather sketchy humans made most prospective check cashers look for a credit card. Fortunately, I had one of those. I decided it was time to make my way up the coast to a town with former friends and a gentle group of scientists and fisher people. Beaufort was a hundred miles away, so I punched out the inlet with no radio or navigational equipment or even an inlet chart for my next landfall.

All I had to do was follow the coast until I spotted Atlantic Beach painted on the local water tower. The Beaufort Inlet was a bit confusing without a chart, but even Blackbeard had his issues with this inlet. He left the *Queen Ann's Revenge* on the offshore bar, and I think he had a chart.

The coast stretched out to the east in an attempt to collide with the north-flowing Gulf Stream. The dune-heaped sandy shoreline swirled and heaved with the incursions of storm tides and long-shore currents. Everything about this coast was about the Stream. Sargassum weed and its ecology of animals drifted along with me and the current toward a reunion with the shores of Carteret County, North Carolina. I had been there before as a transient boater and as a traveling troubadour. Whether by car or by boat, it held a warm place in my soul. A port with happy people still cooking on woodstoves, making wooden instruments and boats, and simply enjoying life.

It was not simple without a chart. I made my approach off-shore to avoid the shallows and breached the ship channel well to the south. Blackbeard had run aground and lost his French prize, the *Queen Anne's Revenge*, somewhere west of the channel, and I did not intend to recreate that scenario on my first attempt. Once in the deep channel, it was easy to follow the numbered buoys into the inner harbor and on into the Beaufort Channel. Rounding the seawall at the Duke Marine Lab, the beautiful antebellum waterfront rims the Taylor Creek shoreline, punctuated with dozens of old sagging wooden docks.

There were only a few boats anchored out, but one stood out as a curiosity worth investigating. It was painted black with a schooner rig. The square yard on the foremast elevated it to brigantine status. Cannons and flags, and the presence of apparently costumed pirates, indicated that something was afoot.

I hailed the master of the vessel, and he replied, "Where ye be from?"

"Key West." I hailed back.

"Are ye here to do battle or would ya care to come to an accord?"

I agreed to the accord and learned that a mock battle between the *Meka Two* and the residents of Beaufort was about to occur. I had been recruited to be part of the incursion on the town, a reenactment, as it were, of a real invasion from the 1700s. The booty was a homemade pie from Mrs. Kell's woodstove. Boy, was it great to be a pie-rate.

A local TV station filmed the pirates rowing ashore in an old lifeboat, growling and arghing, while firing an old rusty swivel gun mounted to the bow of the lifeboat. The townsfolk returned fire with a bronze field-piece cannon on a wheeled carriage. The townsfolk were also armed with pitchforks and axes. We were definitely outgunned and outarmed, and we were repelled and sent running. Of course, this is how Mrs. Kell's history book was written. We followed the history book and proceeded to lose the battle and still eat pie.

After the battle, I decide to take a run at the local bank, not to rob it but hopefully to cash a Florida Keys bank check and replenish my cash levels. The bank was a single-story white clapboard building with a big heavy wooden door. Two hands on the handle, I swung open the door and entered a vestibule fashioned to look a hundred years old. A balding gentleman approached me and offered assistance.

"May I help you? I am Rock Hardison. I'm the manager."

"I'm Ron White, would it be possible to cash an out-of-state check here? I was robbed down the coast, and I'm unable to go on without some cash."

"Where are you bound?"

"Well, I have a biology course scheduled on my boat in Newport, Rhode Island, in ten days."

His eyebrows rose as he motioned to me to follow him. "How much money do you need?"

"Two hundred will do me for the time. In fact, why don't we do a bank transfer, and I will open an account and maybe become a part-time resident."

Rocky leaned back in his chair and said, "Welcome to Beaufort."

I drifted across the street to a lone phone booth right on the edge of the sidewalk. A small wooden dock hosted a few skiffs, probably from the other transients anchored in the harbor. A two-story restaurant was tucked onto the end of the dock. The dock and all the buildings along the two blocks of planked waterfront were new. I was to find out later from Mrs. Kell that Rock Hardison and the mayor, John Costlow, also the director of the Duke Marine Lab, had seques-

Fortunella

tered a grant from the urban renewal grant fund, which fostered the rebuilding of the old Beaufort waterfront. Because the Menhaden industry was slowly petering out, the waterfront was ready for some serious renewal. Instead of thirty large fishing boats tied to the old pier, Beaufort was hoping for a higher class of yacht.

I pulled out my analog address book and punched the number for the professor into the phone at the small Midwestern college, who was supposed to meet me in Newport for a summer marine biology course. Three rings, and the phone picked up. I greeted him and let him know what had happened over the last week and assured him that I would be in Newport on time to meet him and his students.

I finished my train of thought, and he politely interrupted me. "Ron, I'm so sorry, but I could not get enough students together to sanction a course, so we will not need your services this year. Maybe next year."

I have to admit I was not that disappointed. Another five hundred miles into a much-colder climate with lots of fog was weighing on me.

"That's okay, I think I might stay and start an educational sailing business here in Beaufort. There are no charter businesses here right now, and the resource is primed for a nature-tour guy like me."

I hung up the phone and slowly appreciated the landscape of my new home. A small island paralleled the town waterfront. The island was populated by a herd of Spanish ponies. They grazed quietly on the waving seagrass, wetting their lips with the salty tidal water. They dug shallow holes at the tideline and siphoned off the top of the freshwater lens. I turned and noticed a piece of plywood that had washed up with the high tide. I lifted it from the water, brushed off the sand and Sargassum weed, and christened it my new sign.

A block north of Front Street, I passed an ancient cemetery spread behind the church and along the narrow sidewalk. I could not help but notice the grave marker sporting a full-size ship cannon. The stone had a carved name in bold letters, "Otway Burns."

Wow, that is the grave of a famous privateer, I thought. The gate was open, so I went into the live oak grove and sat on a grave next to the cannon. This was real, not a staged set. This was a cannon off the *Snapdragon*, Burns' pirate ship. Stunned, I sat there for a moment and then noticed a northern mockingbird sitting on the cannon. For a reason only the gods know, I reached out with my right hand, and the bird hopped on to my index finger.

Damn, is this a sign? I thought. The bird cocked his head and stood his ground on my finger. Was this a young bird or Captain Burns reaching out from the grave to tell me this was a special place and to stick around? I stuck around.

I stuck around.

Welcome to Beaufort.

Sea Fever

I must go down to the sea again, to the
Vagrant gypsy life,
To the gull's way and the whale's way
Where the wind's like a wetted knife;
And all I ask is merry yarn from a laughing
Fellow rover
And quiet sleep and a sweet dream when
The long trick's over.

John Masefield

ABOUT THE AUTHOR

Captain Ron was born in a navy hospital and attended seven schools on the road to graduation. He graduated from college with a BS in biology and then took marine science courses from six different universities, from New England to Miami. He became a scuba diver in high school and an instructor in college. He taught at the high school and college level in a nursing and repertory therapy school; instructed CPR; and worked at the Mote Marine Lab in Sarasota, Florida; the Environmental Quality Lab in Port Charlotte, Florida; the US Fish and Wildlife Service; and the Foundation for PRIDE in the Turks and Caicos Islands. The foundation was one of the first to offer a resort-based marine ecology course structured for tourists. The course included diving and snorkeling on a magnificent barrier reef and a shallow mangrove swamp. Students were instructed in underwater photography and color-slide developing. The word *ecotourism* had not been coined at that time.

His sailing career started aboard his grandfather's fourteen-foot sailboat. The passion for sail stayed with him, so he bought his first big sailboat, in Mystic, Connecticut, in 1973. Since then, he has sailed over one hundred thousand miles on the East Coast and the Caribbean. He has carried over forty thousand students and passengers on his second sailing vessel, *Good Fortune*, and sponsored forty offshore biological-research expeditions to the Bahamas and the Florida Keys.

9 781638 815716